THE
Creative
LAWYER

THE
Creative
LAWYER

MICHAEL F. MELCHER

**Defending Liberty
Pursuing Justice**

Cover design by ABA Publishing

Printed in the United States of America.

13 12 11   7 6 5

Library of Congress Cataloging-in-Publication Data

Melcher, Michael F.
    The creative lawyer : a practical guide to authentic professional satisfaction / Michael F. Melcher.
        p.   cm.
    Includes index.
    ISBN 978-1-59031-843-0
    1. Practice of law—United States.   2. Lawyers—Job satisfaction—United States.   I. Title.

    KF300.Z9M45 2007

This book is dedicated to
my uncle, Frank Urtuzuástegui, who has shown how to live a creative
life; Jason Mazzone, the creative lawyer I know best;
and to the memory of Astra, the best dog ever

CONTENTS

ACKNOWLEDGMENTS

I am deeply grateful to all the lawyers I interviewed for this book, including many who are not identified in these pages but whose stories and thoughts have helped me to develop the ideas contained herein.

I would like to thank my agent, Molly Lyons of Joëlle Delbourgo Associates, Inc., and my editor, Timothy Brandhorst, for their belief in this project and their ongoing support. Many others offered injections of enthusiasm when I most needed them: Joy Leach, Alyson Alexander, Jennifer Walper, Marci Alboher and most recently Gretchen Rubin. Debby Landesman played a key role on multiple levels in launching my present career.

Throughout my adult life I have benefited from friends who have been believing mirrors for who I am and who I am becoming, especially BFF Faith Adiele, fellow MDL Polly Arenberg, and creative lawyers Henry Robles, Melinda Sarafa, and Cheryl Lappen.

I have learned a great deal from two wise teachers, Clark Freidrichs and Dr. Dror Nir.

Thanks to my parents for the genes, and to my mother in particular for teaching me resourcefulness.

For the last several years I have grown alongside my colleagues at Next Step Partners, for whose company and encouragement I offer thanks, in particular to Rebecca Zucker, my constant airport companion.

My greatest appreciation goes to my clients past and present, including some whose stories I have chronicled here. I cherish their trust and am honored to be part of their continuing journeys.

CHAPTER 1

What Happens Now?

Meet three people.

Jane has practiced law for more than twenty-five years. She worked at a firm and then went in-house at a major bank. She did well and enjoyed her work. After twenty years, a corporate merger eliminated the tight professional team she'd worked and learned with, so Jane decided to explore her long-standing interest in working on issues affecting poor people. She became executive director of a small, regional legal non-profit. But after three years in this new position, Jane feels an awkward mixture of emotions about her career: she loves its purpose, but many of the tasks of being an executive director don't appeal to her. She spends a lot of her time trying to raise money without obvious success, she feels isolated in her office and her support staff is weak. Jane knows how to "think like a lawyer," but thinking like a lawyer isn't helping her figure out what she should do with her life. Should she stick it out or go back into private practice? Has the time for accomplishing great things passed? *What happens now?*

On the opposite side of the experience spectrum is George, who is a junior associate at a big urban law firm. George is moving up in life. He attended a solid college and law school, and his hard work has paid off. George now works at a firm populated with attorneys from many of the Ivy League schools that rejected his earlier applications. Brand recognition is important for George, and he's willing to work hard to keep it and the rewards it will presumably bring. George wants to progress in his career as a lawyer, although ultimately he wants to build a career in business. He also wants to balance his demanding new job with family life—he married three years ago and has a one-year-old child. How will he achieve these disparate goals? He's not sure. Does he just work hard and expect the best? Are there specific strategies he should put into place? Should he plan for the future or focus on the present? *What happens now?*

Several years down the road from George is Nicole. It's been seven years since Nicole finished law school, and she is no longer working as a lawyer. Naturally buoyant, enthusiastic, and filled with ideas, Nicole felt she was not being her real self either in law school or in the three legal jobs she tried after graduating. When her last employer told her that perhaps she should look for alternate employment, she didn't feel depressed. Instead, she experienced a palpable sense of relief. "It was as if I finally had my permission slip to leave. I thought, 'You're right. I'm not the person who should be doing malpractice defense.'"

Nicole spent many months reflecting, exploring, interviewing, and working at various temporary jobs. She ended up taking a job with a large law firm in Los Angeles—but this time working on the firm's marketing efforts. Somewhat to her surprise, she likes her job a lot. She's learning, the salary is decent, and it's a good platform to develop her future. And the nature of that future? Nicole was a dancer for eighteen years, including a stint with a professional company between college and law school. What Nicole really wants to do is to work in entertainment. A vision she has is one day starting her own talent representation agency. But how exactly does she make something like that happen? And how does it square with her current professional path? *What happens now?*

Jane, George, and Nicole are lawyers with different types of experiences, but they face some of the same questions. They want clarity about their goals. They want to know how to achieve them. They want to be successful as professionals and as human beings.

"You're always told that you can do anything with a law degree," says Sayuri Rajapakse, a lawyer in New Jersey. "But the trouble is, people let go of your hand. So you're out there in the world, and you have to figure things out yourself. And that can be complicated."

Why You Need This Book

If you're reading this book, you know a fair amount about the life of a lawyer. But even though you're familiar with the life of a lawyer, there's a lot you still don't know about *your* life and what's going to become of it.

You might be an associate at a megafirm or you might be a city prosecutor. You might be a sole practitioner or part of a large government department. You might be just starting or planning your way out.

Whatever the case, you face one major question, just like Jane, George, and Nicole. *Now what?* It's the question that's always out there.

Your big-picture goals in the end are similar to those of a lot of other people. You want to be happy. You want to be fulfilled. You want to make money, grow, have healthy relationships, express yourself, experience the world. These goals are common. You don't have to be a lawyer to have them.

Yet, whether you're practicing or not, you *are* a lawyer. It's not your identity, but it's one of the things that make up your identity. You have a particular skill set and are likely doing a particular kind of work. You spend a large portion of your time with people who also know this kind of work.

Whatever your particulars, you want to do something about your life and career—something positive. Only you're not sure what that is, or how to do it. That's what this book is all about.

Being the Creative Lawyer

The basic point of this book is to give you one big thing—a different perspective on how to manage your life and career. To use a phrase that appears oxymoronic but is not, I want you to be systematically creative. This means analyzing your desires, interests, temperament, and ambitions. It means designing goals related to things you're sure about and experiments about things you're not. It means mastering the present while anticipating the future.

The creative lawyer is any lawyer who uses his or her own creativity to make a life that works. This can be in law or outside of it.

Why do I use the word *creative*? Because professional satisfaction is a question of creating what you want, not just waiting for it to appear. You become a creative lawyer when you take stewardship of your own life and career.

The specifics of being a creative lawyer are:

1. understanding your own temperament, interests, and values as they actually are
2. assessing realistically how these connect, or don't connect, with the work you do
3. creating a plan for integrating who you are with what you do, making use of a group of tools that will take you from *thinking* to actually *doing*

The point of this book is to show you how to do these things. All of the examples are based on real people, although some names and identifying details have been changed.

3

How This Book Will Help You

If you're a young lawyer, *The Creative Lawyer* will give you a template for envisioning and managing your own professional development. It will help you integrate work and life from the beginning so that your career unfolds in the way you want it to. It will help you get the most out of your investment in a legal education and career.

If you're an experienced lawyer, this book will help you to reassess and renew your career. It will aid you in understanding how your own values and passions might have changed over the years, and what to do if they have. It will give you a method for ensuring that you have balance in your life.

If you are unhappy or stuck in your career, this book will help you figure out ways to ameliorate your problems and gradually get to a place where your work is in synch with who you really are.

If you are happy in your career, *The Creative Lawyer* will help you to manage your career so that you can stay happy.

If you are a complex, interesting person who cannot be easily categorized and are not sure *what* you think about your career, this book is for you, too. It will give you a framework for sorting things out and moving forward amidst ambiguity.

Exercise: Assessing Where You Are Now

This book is intended to help *you*. So let's do a quick check-in. Write your answers to the following questions.

1. What emotions describe your attitude toward your career right now?

   shame, guilt, worthlessness, boredom, frustration, hopelessness; aimless + confused on good days, see a glimmer of hope that I will find my path @ BPJ

2. If your current job paid half your present salary, would you still do it?

   No

3. If your current job paid triple your present salary, would you be happy doing it—and no other job—until you retire?

   No

4. What percentage of your work time is productive?

   Ouch. Horrifidly low.

5. What percentage of your leisure time do you really enjoy?

Interesting to think about — not much. I'm happy at yoga.
Watching a good show with Erik. Pretty much always have a cloud over me.

6. What are three positive things about your current job?

① *Prestige* ② *Nice people, very smart, intellectual* ③ *setting — the building;*

7. What are three negative things about your current job? *being downtown*

① *Not much work, & what I have is not interesting* ② *The billable hour*
is a terrible fit for my working style ③ *constantly burdened by pressure*
from myself to
overwork others'
negative
perceptions
of me

8. What would more senior attorneys say about you?
Seems to have a lot of potential but not productive,
not reliable; lacks initiative

④ *Major one I*
forgot — lack
of associate
development/
mentoring/
guidance

9. What would support staff say about you?
Kind + friendly; Those who know me better would say also
that I'm scattered, always late, behind on turning in
forms, batching my time, etc.

10. If you were forbidden from being a lawyer, what would
you do?
+ the brain

Study psychology; write (probably nonfiction —
maybe books, articles,
essays, memoir; +
poetry)

don't think I would
want to counsel
people; would use it
for writing, or
find some other way
to use it

be an artist
be some type of consultant

CHAPTER 2

20 Minutes a Day

I worked as a lawyer for several years. After I stopped practicing law, I embarked upon a number of career shifts that eventually ended up in my coaching practice, which has given me a good laboratory for investigating the topics analyzed in this book. In my work, I frequently see, up close, phenomena that most people experience only once or twice or a handful of times in their own lives.

I have worked with hundreds of individuals on a one-to-one basis and with thousands of others in workshops. My clients have ranged from CEOs to kids just starting out, from financiers and attorneys to wannabe actors and parents reentering the work force. Much of my coaching work focuses on career coaching, which basically means that a lot of professional people come to me asking, "What should I do with my career?"

Coaching various people at different stages of life and in different careers, I've been able to see the outlines—initially dim and later more defined—of which processes work and which ones don't. I have also seen how intelligent people block themselves from moving forward, especially in their predilection for overthinking and underacting. And, with regard to lawyer and former-lawyer clients in particular, I have developed a good sense of which elements of their situations arise from their identities as lawyers, and which are pretty similar to what most professionals face.

The lawyers I have met are a diverse lot. What they have in common is that they typically lack *resources*. They lack coherent theories for understanding how to create a career. They have no good role models to show them how to create what they want. Furthermore, most of the people they talk to—which includes a lot of blocked, not particularly creative people—are total downers when it comes to the topic of how to create a

[handwritten margin note:] int. – he myst have really good perspective

[handwritten note at bottom:] Very well-said – exactly how I feel. could never have put my finger on it.

good life. The problem, they are told far too often, is that *they are lawyers*. This is *how lawyers are*. It is our *fate*.

This is simply not true.

The Limits of Critical Thinking

The legal field doesn't constrain people's potential. But it does tend to constrain their way of *thinking about* potential.

Lawyers sometimes don't see the possibilities before them, and they therefore don't always act in ways that take advantage of those possibilities. At the extreme, lawyers become the keepers of their own cells, walled off from new ideas and energies. They create a kind of acquired sensory deprivation. And how fun is that?

The core cause of this? Well, it's got a lot to do with issue-spotting.

"Issue-spotting" is identifying potential problems, inconsistencies, and unresolved conflicts. When we spot issues—when we "think like a lawyer"—we take things apart, look for flaws, compare possibilities against evidence, contemplate problems, see cracks in arguments, and contemplate risks.

Lawyers who work for ExxonMobil do this, and so do lawyers with the ACLU. The practice cuts across immigration law, tax law, and any other kind of law. It's the default way of approaching problems.

Issue-spotting is an important legal skill. However, it's deadly when it comes to the process of creating the life you want.

When attorneys apply this kind of thinking to questions of their own careers, they tend to:

- analyze rather than explore
- identify flaws and potential problems
- look for clear precedents
- require solutions of general applicability ("What would work for lawyers?") rather than specific applicability ("What would work for me?")
- demand logical explanations
- be skeptical about possibilities
- defer action in situations of uncertainty
- avoid taking risks

These techniques do not work because, as it happens, the process of attaining career fulfillment is not all that dependent on logic. When it comes to careers, *it's only through action that we acquire relevant information.*

great insight

8

It's the *doing* that builds skills and provides reliable data. It's the exploration that leads to certainty. We imagine we can think our way to insight, but insight is something that frequently shows up only after action has been taken.

Lawyers are often not very aware of the role they play in keeping themselves stuck, because the method they use is completely legitimate in other situations. On the surface, they believe they are thinking things through to their logical, proper conclusion. But what they are doing in fact is staying comfortable with familiar, though ineffective, behavior.

The Big Picture: Creating Your Master Plan

The Creative Lawyer Method is all about action. It involves breaking things down into discrete, actionable chunks and *doing* rather than *thinking*. Therefore, the value added by this book is in the doing, not the reading. If you only read it, you probably will not get much out of it. On the other hand, if you do the exercises and actions recommended, I guarantee that you will gain clarity, focus, and ultimately enthusiasm for your career. Sometimes this will feel messy. But it works.

What are the specific factors that make up a fulfilling career?

- The degree of match between your core values and what you do
- Vision and strategy
- Attention to relationships and consistent networking
- Mindful communications
- A habit of experimentation
- Parallel growth and lifelong learning
- A willingness to tolerate ambiguity
- Shaping your own story
- Openness to interrogating personal taboos

The chapters of this book are arranged more or less according to these complementary themes. As you work through the book, you'll do exercises that illustrate how these show up in your life. By the end, you'll have the elements of your own personal master plan. You will have a sense of how it all fits together, and what you need to do.

In the appendix there is a blank template for your plan. The details that will enrich it will come from the exercises you do throughout this book. The appendix also gives three examples of what it might look like completely filled out.

The Details: 20 Minutes a Day on Your Career
(Not *in* Your Career)

If you spend all day doing your job, you'll never get anywhere!

If you want your career to be something other than a hamster wheel, you need to work on yourself with as much dedication as you work on your job—not the same amount of time, but with the same passion. You need to invest time in yourself, every day.

Numerous authors who write about companies or executive performance have made this or very similar points. They range from Stephen Covey, the author of *The 7 Habits of Highly Effective People*, to Paul Orfalea, the founder of Kinko's and author of the book *Copy This!* If you don't work "on" your business (or "on" your career), you will be consumed with the day-to-day grind and never see, understand, or deal with the broader strategic issues at hand.

Everyone knows this, sort of. "*Obviously*," you might be thinking, "I *know* that it's important to reflect, plan, think, strategize, and establish priorities. I'll get to all that just as soon as I have time."

The problem is that you will *never* have time. As long as working *on* your career is something you do after you've finished working *in* your career, you won't make progress. You can't define the project of making the life you want as something that only happens in residual time.

The only way to make time for working on your career is to make it your top priority—to pay attention to yourself first, before anything else. It's the 20-Minutes-a-Day Plan. Devote 20 minutes a day to working on your career. Everything else happens after that.

Here are the basic principles behind the 20-Minutes-a-Day Plan:

1. *If you don't commit to working on your career, you probably won't.*
2. *You can accomplish useful activities in 20 minutes that will make meaningful contributions to your long-term happiness and success.*
3. *You can always find 20 minutes in your day.*

Let me repeat that last one: *You can always find 20 minutes in your day.* I swear.

What can you do in 20 minutes? *A LOT*. The following list gives some examples of how you can use 20 minutes a day to enrich your career.

None of these count as real, billable work. But they all contribute to your success or happiness or both. In subsequent chapters, we'll go into detail about the different ways into the process of creating a fulfilling career. In the meantime, add some additional 20-minute activities in the blank spaces. Then circle the items you find most appealing.

10

Exploration and future vision

- Do most of the exercises in this book
- Conduct one informational phone interview
- Conduct one short, formal interview
- Attend one networking coffee session
- Send one well-written cover email
- Write one quick draft of a one-year plan
- Write one quick draft of a thirty-year plan
- Write about your dream – where you
- work on a "vision board" / some sort of visual depiction

would truly want to be in 6,10,15,20

Learning and research

- Skim forty to fifty pages of a nonfiction book
- Read eight to ten pages in depth
- Conduct five to ten Google searches
- Conduct one research session on amazon.com
- Locate / read articles on relevant topics
- Identify & list organizations, etc. of interest to you

Professional development

- Attend 1/3 of a professional learning presentation
- Have two short interactions at a professional event
- Fill out one online application to attend a conference
- Do several practices of your positioning statement
- look into Inns of court
- schedule lunches w/ partners

? ←

Business development

- Send five short emails (e.g., thank-you notes or appointment-setting emails)
- Make one quick network assessment
- Do one or two telephone check-ins with clients
- Leave five to ten voicemails for people who aren't there
- Do one quick review of your résumé or bio
- work on my Outlook contacts
- organize list of friends / acquaintances / contacts

• review local publications for ideas – who might need a lawyer / what kind of new things are happening in Memphis? (related to)

11

- Talk to M. Hamm re: "start-up" idea
- List substantive expertise req. for

Physical balance

- Take one head-clearing walk outside
- Do one short cardio workout
- Purchase a meal from outside
- Make and pack lunch
- Eat one meal alone, calmly, without multitasking
- Attend 1/3 of a massage, training session, or yoga class
- _plan dinners for week_
- _prep healthy b-fast for next morning (smoothie, for ex.)_

Emotional and psychic balance

○ gardening

- Glance through an entire newspaper
- Read one chapter of a good novel
- Make one personal journal entry
- Enjoy one chatty phone call with a good friend
- Make four quick check-in calls with loved ones
- Place two gift orders online
- Write, address, and stamp one card or note
- _Read a magazine_
- _Home organization / purging_

Work management

○ visual reminders –
– each project
– deadline calendar

- Write one daily plan or well-structured "to-do" list
- Frame or hang one picture (to personalize your office)
- Purchase flowers (to brighten your office)
- Clear one cluttered surface
- Rearrange one drawer
- Have one informal but meaningful feedback session with boss or subordinate
- _work on my files – scanning, recycling, etc._
- _work on my email organization_

Exercise: Plan Your Next Ten 20-Minute Sessions

Doing something consistently for two weeks starts to make it a habit. List ten things from the above list you can commit to doing in the next ten days. Identify the dates you will do these things. As you actually perform these things, check them off.

1. Action _____ Date _____

2. Action _____ Date _____

3. Action _____ Date _____

4. Action _____ Date _____

5. Action _____ Date _____

6. Action _____ Date _____

7. Action _____ Date _____

8. Action _____ Date _____

9. Action _____ Date _____

10. Action _____ Date _____

Exercise: Make Your Pledge

Fill in the blanks below. Then make a copy of your pledge and post it in a place where you will run into it repeatedly, like on top of your computer screen, above your car radio, or on your refrigerator door.

I, _____, pledge to commit 20 minutes a day to working on my career. I will do this every day at _____. If for some reason I miss it, I will make it up _____. This contract is enforceable in every jurisdiction in the world.

ADDITIONAL EXERCISES
Exercise: Investing in Your Life

What's at stake for you? What are the potential benefits? Write answers to the following questions.

1. How many *years* have you invested in your legal career (include school and years working)? _____

2. How much *money* have you spent developing this career? $_____

3. How many more years do you expect to work in your life? _____

4. On a scale of 1 to 100, how would you rate your current overall level of *career satisfaction*? _____

5. On a scale of 1 to 100, how would you rate your current overall level of *personal satisfaction*? _____

6. How would you feel if you could substantially raise either or both of those satisfaction numbers? _____

7. What percentage of waking time are you willing to devote to improving your life? _____

Exercise: Identify Your Time Bogs

It's easier to carve out 20 minutes a day if you are aware of when you are wasting time. And it's easier to limit these unproductive activities if you are aware of the things that trigger them.

List your time-wasting activities. To start, list five ways that you waste time during the workday. Examples: Checking political blogs during the day; standing in line to buy food instead of bringing it from home; taking calls from relatives who you know will just complain for fifteen minutes; participating in meetings that start late and end late.

1. Waste of time _____
2. Waste of time _____
3. Waste of time _____
4. Waste of time _____
5. Waste of time _____

List triggering situations. Now, list the situations that these trigger time-wasting activities. Examples: I'm more likely to waste time when I take calls directly rather than letting my secretary screen them; I'm more likely to waste time when I'm late to meetings myself, therefore letting

14

other people get away with being late; I'm more likely to waste time when I don't take regular breaks to recharge.

1. I'm more likely to waste time when _____

_____

_____

2. I'm more likely to waste time when _____

_____

_____

3. I'm more likely to waste time when _____

_____

_____

4. I'm more likely to waste time when _____

_____

_____

5. I'm more likely to waste time when _____

_____

_____

Take positive action. With the goal of freeing up 20 minutes a day to do things that will really benefit your career, write out five actions you can take that will eliminate some or most of these triggering situations. Examples: Get out the door by 7:30 a.m. to avoid traffic; only read emails at the top of the hour, not each time they come in; take a mental health break every two hours.

1. Action _____

2. Action _____

3. Action _____

4. Action _____

5. Action _____

READING LIST

One enriching thing you can do as part of your 20-Minutes-a-Day Plan is to read (not for every single session, but for some). There are a lot of great books out there that speak intelligently on the processes of managing career fulfillment. I'll offer suggestions according to topic area throughout this book. In terms of general overviews, consider the following.

The Big Picture

Daniel Pink, *A Whole New Mind*

Pink was a speechwriter for Al Gore before he wrote his first book, *Free Agent Nation*, which examined the degree to which new models of self-employment are changing our economy and society. Now solidly established as a trend-spotter, Pink has come up with a convincing theory that the true growth area in careers are those that combine left-brain and right-brain skills. This book is especially relevant to knowledge workers who come from left-brain dominant fields like law, medicine, accounting, and computer programming. A wake-up call and an inspiration.

Mihalyi Csikszentmihalyi, *Finding Flow*

Want to know how fulfillment works? Csikszentmihalyi explains it, focusing on "the psychology of everyday engagement" and applying decades of research. Csikszentmihalyi argues that fulfillment is under the control of individuals, as opposed to happiness, which is more affected by external variables. One of his great findings is that people are far more fulfilled at work than at leisure. An academic writer whose insights are readable, relevant, and based on solid research.

Working and Living More Effectively

David Allen, *Getting Things Done*

Allen, a productivity expert, goes into great detail about specifically how you should manage time and tasks. Usually when reading getting-things-done type books, I skim. This one, I read every page.

Talane Miedaner, *Coach Yourself to Success*

One hundred and one coaching tips to improve your life—and the tips really work. This is a favorite of many of my clients, especially those who are "sensing types" on the Myers-Briggs Type Indicator (see chapter 7). As my client Tony put it, "Extremely useful and uplifting, but not in a powdered-donut way."

CHAPTER 3

Who You Are *Now*: Identifying Your Values

I once met a famous politician. He had worked in politics all of his adult life and had attained one of the handful of elected positions in the United States that connote real power before resigning after a personal scandal. I liked this politician a lot and was thrilled that, when I met him at a book signing, he took me seriously as an interesting, accomplished person. We agreed to meet later to have a real conversation.

"So, Michael," the famous politician started off, "What should I do with my career?"

I was surprised to be asked this. It hadn't occurred to me that someone of his age and background would want my opinion about his career.

I started with a standard slow pitch. "Okay, tell me what's going on with your career."

The FP held forth. What was going on was: he had followed a very clear professional path for most of his life, seeking ever higher political office. Now that he had left elected politics, that clarity was gone. Professionally, he didn't know who he was anymore.

"Well, what do you want to do with your career?" I asked.

"To give back," he said. "To make a difference."

"Okay," I said, "how do you want to make a difference? What interests you most?"

He named two of the issues he felt most passionate about.

"Those are good issues," I said. "But how would you like to affect these issues? What do you actually want to *do*?"

"Just, you know, make a difference. Make a contribution." The FP paused. "So what should I do?"

I sensed we were hitting a wall. So I asked more questions, most of them beginning with the word *what* or *how*. "What is it that excites you about these issues?" "How do you like to work with people?" "What role would you like to play?" All of these were very difficult for him to answer.

The famous politician had a general label for the life he wanted, but he hadn't dug any deeper. And because he had not disaggregated the elements that were important to him, he was running a risk of entering something he wouldn't like and possibly wouldn't do well at.

He had performed many different functions during his decades in politics—candidate for public office, legislator, policy analyst, fundraiser, speech maker, deal maker—but he hadn't thought about what he liked or didn't like about these particular functions. They were all bundled together under the labels "politics" and "public service."

I drilled down to see how he pictured the reality of one of the jobs he was exploring—being a sort of in-house policy maker for a major foundation.

"So does that mean you want to attend lots of meetings? Deal with the board of directors in a closed room all day?"

"No!"

"Do you want to sit at the phone, dialing for dollars?"

"No! I'd hate that."

"Would you like to be out in the field, visiting schools or community organizations or nonprofits, interacting with people on the ground, folks of all ages?"

"Yes, that's what I want to do, Michael," he said, excited.

"Do you want to give speeches or have more intimate meetings with individuals or small groups?"

"Both," he said. "I love all that."

The famous politician had started to identify some of his values—things that he wanted in his life. We already knew he wanted to make a contribution. Now we also knew that he wanted to work directly with people, do public speaking, and be out in the world, not stuck in the office. He was energized by diversity—connecting with people of all types, from school kids to suits.

"So what should I do? Which job is that?"

"I don't know," I said. "That's something we can figure out. But I think it would be helpful to look at who you are apart from the titles you've had. That's the first step. Looking at who you are *now*."

A person's career experience is always individual. Put ten different people into the same job and they'll experience it ten different ways. What practicing law (or not practicing law) actually means to you depends on who you are. Career satisfaction comes from a match between who you are and what you do.

Who you are is a combination of many factors. It depends on your values, interests, and ambitions. It depends on how your personality works and how you prefer to navigate the world. And it depends on the kinds of visions you pursue.

Law will neither make your identity nor erase it.

When Do You Like Being You?

Let's start with a simple question. When do you like being you? Everyone has his own answer.

When I'm learning something new.
When I'm in nature.
When I'm part of a team.
When I'm running a deal.
When I'm being an advocate.
When I'm writing something good.
When I'm by myself.
When I'm in a foreign country.
When I'm helping someone.
When I'm cashing my paycheck.
When I'm seeing my kids.
When I'm playing with my dogs.
When I see my name in lights.

Asking "When do you like being you?" is a way of asking: What are your values?

Values are the qualities that make our lives compelling, interesting, and fulfilling. They are the elements that enable us to thrive. Values are not the same thing as morals or ethics. They're not what you're *supposed* to like. They're what you *do* like. Living your values doesn't mean doing the right things. It means doing the things that make you feel right.

There are hundreds of values. A selection is listed at the end of this chapter. Each person's preferred set is different. And the ones you have now may not be the ones you grew up with. Your values are whatever you have the itch for. Recognition! Fun! Solitude! Accomplishment! Leisure! Spirituality! Money!

A core principle of coaching is that if you are consistently happy, it is probably because you are living a life that manifests your core values. Conversely, if you feel consistently frustrated, angry, or trapped, then you are probably not living your values; your life is an ill-fitting suit, not tailored to who you are.

Because we live in a culture that emphasizes validation through external approval, many people have never really asked themselves what things in life are truly important to them. They're not sure what their values are. But these values are quite easy to discover. They lie just under the surface. We'll do several exercises to investigate what your values are.

Your Peak Experiences

One way to uncover your values is to examine some of your peak experiences. A peak experience is one in which you feel totally alive and engaged in what you are doing. During peak experiences, people feel deeply focused and often lose track of time. A person feels, in the language of psychologist Mihalyi Csikszentmihalyi, a sense of "flow." Oftentimes during a peak experience, you may not be aware that an activity is particularly pleasurable—it's when you finish that you feel a sense of deep fulfillment. A peak experience can be pure fun or require extreme effort—either way, when you're finished you think, "That was fantastic!"

A peak experience may last five minutes or two years. For one person, a peak experience might come when slaloming down a mountain; for another, when caring for an infant; for a third, when writing a tax treatise; and for yet another, when performing stand-up comedy. Your peak experience might be a reflection of your public self, or it may manifest a secret self that few are aware of.

I often ask clients about their peak experiences.

Mona, an attorney, talked about a time when she worked in the Treasury Department. "I worked on anti–money laundering efforts, so I traveled a lot overseas. One of the most significant experiences was when I went to Kuwait.

"Throughout the Middle East, a huge number of the workers and servants are South Asians, like me—from India, Pakistan, Bangladesh, Sri Lanka. I had sort of known that before going over, but it was very unsettling when I first got there. I was part of the American delegation but people initially seemed to think I was a kind of assistant. At the hotel, they'd refer to me by my first name while calling my colleagues by their last names, and so forth.

"But I was part of the delegation, and so I'd show up at diplomatic events and jaws would just drop. I was young, still in my twenties. And

I was a woman, and brown, and actually representing the U.S. government in international negotiations.

"The American Foreign Service people hosting us were bursting with smugness and self-satisfaction because I was proof positive that America is just better. That made me feel a little strange. But then I saw how the South Asians working there reacted. Their faces literally lit up when they saw me. The cooks and servers and laborers were ecstatic that I was actually there as a lawyer with the American delegation. I got extra helpings of everything because they were so pleased and proud.

"So, I felt I was representing the United States government and the American dream, and I was also representing South Asia. I was an example of what could happen if South Asians were actually given educational opportunities and freedom, especially women. It reminded me of how important it is to me to be a professional woman. I saw that there were so many other South Asian woman who never had the opportunities I did—and they might have been very brilliant but had no outlet."

I asked Mona what values she saw. What did this peak experience say about the things that are important to her? (The italics are mine, to emphasize the values.)

"Well, for one, *living up to my potential* is important, making something out of my education. And obviously I like *travel*. And not just travel, being in *international and multicultural environments*. It's something that I like and something that I'm good at. And I do like *challenges*—not quite knowing if I have what it takes, doing things that are actually a little scary. I do my best under those circumstances. I like working with other *smart people*. I liked having *expertise* in a particular area—I really knew what those policies were. Something I also see is that I'm a real believer in *meritocracy*—I was young, but because I could do the work, I was put out in front. I can tell you that when I'm not in a meritocracy—like my current job—I really wither."

"When I think about those experiences," she continued, "I realize that I actually like being a lawyer. I'm still completely frustrated and unhappy at my current legal job, and there were some things I didn't like about the Treasury job, but I can see how certain aspects of being a lawyer really connect with who I am."

Exercise: Your Peak Experiences

In the spaces below, write a few sentences about two of your peak experiences. (Try to make at least one of them non–work related.) Don't worry about articulating your values at first—concentrate on describing the details. If you wish, answer the following questions to get you started:

> What happened?
> How did you feel?
> What was good about it?
> What skills did you use?
> What feedback did you get?

Peak experience #1:

_____

_____

_____

_____

_____

_____

_____

_____

Peak experience #2:

_____

_____

_____

_____

_____

_____

_____

_____

Now, read over what you've done. Imagine that you're meeting the person who wrote these for the first time. Based on the stories you've written, what values are important to this person? Jot down as many potential values as you can. Don't worry about which is most important or how they connect to your career or the rest of your life. Examples might include *international connections, expertise, challenge,* or *working with intelligent people.*

Value _____   Value _____

Value _____   Value _____

Value _____   Value _____

Value _____   Value _____

Value _____   Value _____

This is a working list. In the next few exercises, we'll add more values and get a sense of the ones that are most important to you. Then we'll talk about what you do with this knowledge.

Exercise: Interest Questionnaire

Values show up in the ways you express your interests. Quickly answer the following questions.

1. What parts of the newspaper do you read first? _____
   _____
   _____

2. What are three books you've read in the past year? _____
   _____
   _____

3. As a child, what did you do in your free time? _____
   _____
   _____

4. What's a goal that has been on your list for a few years? _____
   _____
   _____

5. What's a life you haven't lived? _____
   _____
   _____

6. What are your hobbies? _____
   _____
   _____

7. What types of activities energize you? _____
   _____
   _____

8. What do you like to be in charge of? _____

_____

_____

9. Which famous people intrigue you? _____

_____

_____

10. What about those people do you respect? _____

_____

_____

Review your answers to the questions above. What additional values do these answers suggest?

Value _____   Value _____

Value _____   Value _____

Value _____   Value _____

Value _____   Value _____

Value _____   Value _____

Evaluating Your *Shoulds*

Clarifying your values involves crossing out as well as adding. For most of us, our goals are partly our own design and partly the internalization of messages about what we *should* want. We may carry around beliefs for decades without actually asking if they are relevant to our own experiences and desires.

"Shoulds" get in the way of fulfillment. They use up energy, distract us from our true interests, and block us from taking action.

Consider some of the following shoulds:

- I've devoted a lot of years to a specialty, so I shouldn't give it up now.
- Since I spent all that money going to law school, I shouldn't just throw it away.
- I should stay home with my children.
- I should make as much money as my law school classmates.
- My wife shouldn't be earning more than I am.

- I should pick one thing and just stick to it.
- I should become an investment banker.
- I should make partner.
- I should see foreign films instead of watching *American Idol*.
- I should stick it out in my awful job rather than disrupting my family's lives.

Exercise: List Your Shoulds

In the space below, write down some of your shoulds.

1. I should _____
2. I should _____
3. I should _____
4. I should _____
5. I should _____
6. I should _____
7. I should _____
8. I should _____
9. I should _____
10. I should _____

Exercise: Your Restatement of Shoulds

You don't have to accept your shoulds at face value. This is a great place to use your ability to think like a lawyer to do some critical analysis. Consider how certain shoulds could be analyzed and restated:

Original Shoulds	Restatement of Shoulds
I should stay home with my children.	I love my children and am a good parent. But that doesn't mean I want to stay home with my kids. I would rather be a positive example of how to balance family and career.
I should become an investment banker.	I have no interest in finance, and I am not sufficiently compelled by money to do something I don't want to do.

Take five of the shoulds you've described above and write more sophisticated versions where you distinguish what is true and not true about them.

1. I _____

   _____

   _____

2. I _____

   _____

   _____

3. I _____

   _____

   _____

4. I _____

   _____

   _____

5. I _____

   _____

   _____

Exercise: What's Important to You—*Now*

Take another look at the exercises you've just done and the values list included at the end of this chapter and ask yourself: What are my core values? Pick six to ten.

My values:

1. _____
2. _____
3. _____
4. _____
5. _____
6. _____
7. _____
8. _____
9. _____
10. _____

MP

Master Plan Intervention!

Copy your top values over to your Master Plan (see appendix).

Examples of Values

The following list gives numerous examples of values that are important to different people.

Action	Freedom	Productivity
Adventure	Friendship	Professionalism
Advocacy	Fun	Public policy
Ambition	Health	Rationality
Animals	Home	Recognition
Appreciation	Honesty	Relationships
Art	Humor	Religion
Autonomy	Idealism	Respect
Balance	Influence	Risk
Beauty	Inspiration	Sensuality
Building	Intellectual	Service
Business	stimulation	Sex
Challenge	International	Social change
Children	Language	Solitude
Communication	Leadership	Spirituality
Community	Legacy	Sports
Compassion	Legal achievement	Stability
Competition	Mastery	Status
Contribution	Mentoring	Stimulation
Control	Money	Success
Diligence	Nature	Superiority
Diversity	Order	Synthesizing
Education	Originality	Teaching
Ethics	People	Team
Excellence	Persuasion	membership
Excitement	Philanthropy	Travel
Experimentation	Physical	Variety
Expertise	fitness	Winning
Fame	Politics	Wealth
Family	Popularity	Work
Financial stability	Practicality	Writing

READING LIST: BOOKS ON CREATIVITY

Books on creativity are great ways to probe deeply into your core values. These books are all about getting in tune with who you really are rather than who you think you are supposed to be.

Twyla Tharp, *The Creative Habit: Learn It and Use It for Life*

Choreographer Twyla Tharp has written a book about all types of creativity. Her book is a compelling how-to manual for developing creative practices. Creativity is often perceived as something that comes as inspiration; Tharp shows how it's the product of sustained effort.

Julia Cameron, *The Artist's Way*
Julia Cameron, *The Right to Write*
Julia Cameron, *The Vein of Gold*

Ten years after first reading *The Artist's Way*, I still turn to it at least once a week and each time find something useful. Cameron's books are directed to "shadow artists"—people with creative impulses who tend to believe that only other people, not themselves, count as real artists. Her books are supportive and insightful guides to awakening your creativity and taking your desires for an improved life seriously. Her two basic tools, the "Morning Pages" and the "Artist's Date," will improve the quality of anyone's life.

Sandra Tsing Loh, *A Year in Van Nuys*

And now for something completely different—one of the funniest books I've ever read. Loh, a comic writer and contributor to National Public Radio, examines the mental state of someone in her thirties who is not sufficiently successful, productive, thin, or spiritually advanced. The real subject is figuring how to live life on your own terms when the world isn't cooperating. (The title is a takeoff on Peter Mayle's *A Year in Provence*. As Loh says in the opening, "Not only do I not live in Provence, I don't even live in a nice part of Los Angeles.")

CHAPTER 4

Living Your Values in Work and Life

Theories of Balance

When people give advice on how to achieve the widely desired but somewhat opaque goal of work/life balance, they often end up expounding on one of two topics. The first is time management. Any airport bookstore features numerous books about how to manage your time and priorities more effectively (such as by reading self-help books during boring airplane flights). The message is that if you can accomplish your work requirements in less time, you will have more time for your personal activities and therefore be more balanced.

Though I love being efficient, the time-management theory of work/life balance does not do much for me. Balance through efficient scheduling does not sound enticing or even sustainable to me.

The second frequently discussed topic is boundaries. Work/life balance requires skills like "saying no," "establishing limits," "setting boundaries," and "standing up for yourself." I certainly agree with this. If you can't say no, or if you say no in a way that sounds like "yes" or "maybe," you have a problem.

The trouble is, I've rarely seen people achieve work/life balance just by setting boundaries. Setting boundaries works for a time. But much like the Dutch in an epoch of global warming, you'll have to keep going back to plug those dikes. The pressures for you to work and produce will just keep piling on, *unless* . . .

Unless what?

Unless there are countervailing forces!

In my view, the way you achieve optimal balance is by building up the things that are important to you. You do this by recognizing, loving, and cultivating your values. You give them enough attention that they can emerge as forces in their own right and become as insistent a power within your consciousness as work. If you are faced with the Godzilla of work, don't battle it alone. Enlist Rodan to even out the contest.

Good time management is helpful. Setting boundaries is essential. But what really makes balance sustainable is inviting your values into your life.

Lessons from Child Rearing

The clearest example of how this dynamic works is in the realm of child rearing. What happens to people when they have kids and continue to work? Most of the time, they become more efficient. A *lot* more efficient.

Julie Chodos has spent most of her time since law school working in marketing and sales. At the time we spoke, her child was six months old and Julie was continuing to work full-time.

"I'm much more efficient now," she said. "If I thought I multitasked well before, I multitask a hundred times better now. I'm better able to live in the moment because when I'm at work I'm very focused on what I have to do at work. Once I'm out of the office, I'm focused on what I have to do at home."

Part of Julie's focus comes from a realization that perfection in either working or parenting is impossible, if for no other reason than limited time. She was somewhat surprised that her life now is less stressful, rather than more so.

"Before I had my daughter, I really wasn't sure how I'd handle it," she admitted. "I wasn't sure how being a parent would affect things. But actually it just made everything 100 percent better. I don't have the luxury of sitting and agonizing over certain things anymore. I just don't. My husband and I are both very conscientious about how we approach our jobs, but we both have a much better perspective on work and home than we ever did before."

Julie did not wait for her work life to contain itself before she had a child. It was the entrance of the child into their lives that stimulated her and her husband to create balance.

Deb Swenson, a partner in a Minneapolis bankruptcy firm, became the primary parent of her twelve-year-old nephew, Rob, soon after she graduated from Stanford Law School. Deb had done well in challenging situations before. Visually impaired, she lived for years in public housing before deciding to go to college in her late thirties. She sailed through the University of Minnesota and then attended Stanford Law, graduating in 1995. Still, she was not sure how she would succeed as a parent or as a lawyer.

What gave Deb guidance was a clear sense of what was important to her.

"My priorities changed after I realized Rob was going to be in my life forever," she says. "He became the number one priority. It wasn't me anymore, and it wasn't work anymore. It was him."

Since neither work nor parenting was optional, Deb made the balance happen.

"I'd go to work, and each night when I'd come home, he'd be there with my law school flash cards, wanting to do a little quiz. Although he was in junior high school, he was into that for some reason. On weekends, we would go to the office and he'd do his homework in the conference room and call his friends while I'd do my work, and then we'd go out to eat." ○

At a certain point, the firm she had been working at—which she'd joined partly for quality-of-life issues—became significantly more demanding. It became harder to spend time with her nephew, who was then in high school. "We solved that by hiring him. He'd come in after school to do filing and other tasks. That way we at least got to be in the same place."

Now, years down the road, Deb feels good both about her career as a respected bankruptcy counsel and about the child she raised, a six-foot-three college graduate who is now working in New York and (surprise, surprise) studying for the LSAT.

It's not only people raising children whose values impel them to find balance. It's anyone who knows what his or her passions are and lets them bloom.

Mona, whom we met in chapter 3, is still working as an attorney but is also pursuing an arts administration program on weekends at a local university. In her classmates, she's seen how clarity on values can affect the choices one makes. Her program includes people who have been dancers, visual artists, and museum curators; people who have worked in managerial and fundraising roles in the arts; and folks from other careers entirely.

"You talk to lawyers, and many of them are achingly discontented," Mona says. "Yet in a way they accept discontent. Whereas the people I've met in these courses, whether they come from the visual arts or management, do not accept discontent. They are not making a great living financially, but they're making a living that contents them. Because they're doing exactly what they want."

She continues: "They still have tradeoffs. They may be in the back office of some tiny little museum, or they have to spend hours each day fundraising. Some of them want to move into something totally different. But generally speaking, they are content with their choices. They want to be in the arts. It's worth it to them."

When you fully express your values, the overall shape of your life changes. Some things become more important, and others less so. Living your values fully doesn't mean that work will no longer be important or demanding. Nor does it mean that you won't need, like, or desire money. But when you invest in your values, you force yourself to draw on your creative powers to find ways to make the overall mix work better.

How Close Are You?

Are you currently living a life that expresses your values?

Let's look at how your life looks now.

Figure 4-1 is a commonly used coaching tool. Each of the eight slices represents a core value. In the example, a particular individual has identified core values of financial security, lifelong learning, recognition, family connections, physical fitness and health, creativity, competition, and civic/community contribution.

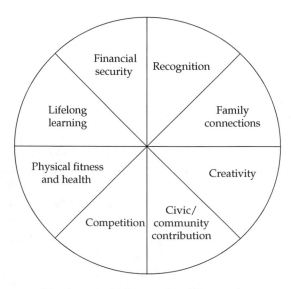

Figure 4-1. Values Wheel Example

32

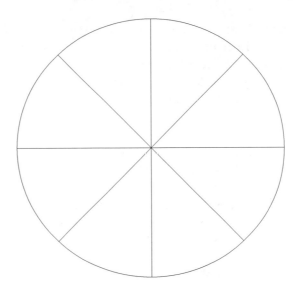

Figure 4-2. Your Values Wheel

Now let's do your version. On the blank wheel in figure 4-2, write in eight of your top values.

Next, on a scale of 1 to 10, assess the extent to which you are living each of your values, with 1 being "almost nonexistent" and 10 being "fully manifesting the value in my life." Write each of these numbers on the corresponding section of the circle.

Now, considering the center of the circle to be 0 and the perimeter to be 10, draw a line in each section to represent the numerical score for each of your values. This is your "values wheel." Ideally, you should have a smooth, round, large wheel. Since life is not ideal, however, most people end up with wheels that are unbalanced, with some values flourishing and others dormant at best.

Which of your values are being expressed? Which ones are not?

Creating a Values Fulfillment Plan

We're going to pose two questions now for each of your values:

1. What would your life be like if the expression of this value in your life were a 10?
2. What can you do *now* to move the value closer to a 10—even if it's just moving from 3 to 3.5?

One of Jeanne-Marie's values was *international connections*. Jeanne-Marie loved travel and languages. She had grown up speaking both

33

French and English at home, and later had studied both Italian and Spanish to a high degree of fluency. Her year abroad in Barcelona during college was one of the high points of her life.

In recent years, Jeanne-Marie had been working in Seattle with no particular international focus. She and her husband had a two-year-old daughter and were expecting a second child. Jeanne-Marie missed her international connections value.

"Sometimes it's hard for me to accept that I'm here, living in a duplex in Seattle," she said. "I have this idea that we'll all go and live in France, but it seems very impractical now and for the next several years. I feel good about my decisions, but I also feel a real loss for that part of me." Jeanne-Marie rated herself a 5 for international connections.

"What would a 10 look like?" I asked.

"If I had a 10 for international connections, our whole family would be living in France, probably in Normandy where my mom grew up. Or maybe we'd live in Paris but have a weekend cottage in Normandy. My kids would be totally bilingual. Dylan would be working at a great job that he loved in Paris, and I would be working, as well, although perhaps I'd be an entrepreneur of some kind rather than working for a company. Maybe my business would have something to do with creating business connections between the U.S. and France. When I think of it, it's not that I want to become French. I just want to feel international, every single day of my life."

"So, what are some things you might do to get closer to a 10?" I asked.

"Just random things?" she asked.

"Yes, just random things. You don't have to choose anything right now."

"Well, I could hook up with other parents who are trying to raise their kids to be bilingual," she said. "I actually know one other couple, and I'm sure there are others. And I could look into what resources there are for that—bilingual preschools, or classes, or activity groups. We already have a bilingual caregiver," she added.

"Really?" I hadn't known that.

"Yes, he's great. He's from Rwanda and was educated in Paris. His French is wonderful."

"That's totally cool," I said.

"I have to agree," Jeanne-Marie replied. "Maybe I should raise my score from 5 to 6. I had forgotten how I arranged that."

After some additional brainstorming, Jeanne-Marie identified several ways of being more international, short of moving her entire family to France and finding dream jobs. The ideas she came up with included:

- Seeing more foreign films
- Taking Spanish classes at a local college
- Decorating her home with more of an international theme
- Learning how to use Skype so she could easily call friends around the world
- Connecting with a civic organization focused on international events
- Making a point of inviting over colleagues at work who were from foreign countries and who had limited ties in the United States

"Which ones do you most want to pursue now?" I asked. "What can you commit to?"

"I want to learn Skype! I'm way behind on technology and would like to see how this could add to my life."

This is how you start living your values—and frankly, how you begin to achieve balance. Not through giant leaps, but by baby steps.

Exercise: Brainstorming Your Values Plan

On a separate page, create a chart similar to the one below. For each of your values, determine what a 10 would look like. Then brainstorm at least three steps you could take right now to incorporate your values more into your life. Circle the ones that you want to commit to first.

MY VALUES PLAN

Value	What a 10 would look like	Three steps I can take now
Financial freedom (current score: 3)	No worries, healthy retirement fund, robust college accounts for kids.	1. Make appointment with financial planner. 2. Drink coffee at home or work, rather than going to Starbucks every day. 3. Talk to Lee about the financial seminar she went to.
Physical fitness (current score: 4.5)	I eat well, do yoga every day, and play intramural football each fall. I relish life.	1. Start cooking at home three nights per week. 2. Yoga two times a week. 3. Check Web for open sports leagues in town.
Value		
Value		
Value		
Value		
Value		

CHAPTER 5

Be Clear about Your Tradeoffs

The Unlikely Story of Betsy Chao

Betsy Chao is a top lawyer in the China market. A partner in a major national law firm, she is a key advisor to Chinese companies and U.S. financial institutions. She knows the law, is highly experienced in transactions, and has a vast personal network across the Pacific Rim. Betsy is in great demand.

Because Betsy is so established in her current career and because she looks at least ten or fifteen years younger than she really is, most people do not realize that she had a whole other career before she became a super pan-Asia deal maker. In fact, "career" understates matters—she had another life entirely.

For more than twenty years, starting in college and continuing into the years just prior to law school, Betsy was a political activist. She was part of "the Movement." In college, she was a leader in Students for a Democratic Society and spoke at rallies across the country. She later worked as an organizer of farm workers and garment workers. She ran a community organization in San Francisco's Chinatown and was a key player in Jesse Jackson's two presidential campaigns.

Betsy used to be known for things like hanging out with the Black Panthers. Now she is known for things like flying from Washington, D.C., to Beijing, holding an eight-hour meeting, and flying right back.

How does one square the different sides of Betsy Chao? The investment-banking lawyer with the campus activist? The international deal maker with the workers' rights organizer?

One resolves these questions by starting with the idea that Betsy, like all of us, is an individual. And as an individual, she has many potential identities, all legitimate. She proves the point made by Herminia Ibarra, the author of *Working Identity*, that we each have multiple potential selves. To connect this idea with our previous discussion about values, Betsy's two careers might be different manifestations of the same values, or they may reflect different values entirely.

In the earlier part of her life, Betsy was driven by values that included justice, community development, being part of a larger movement, intellectual discourse, doing things that were real, and being connected to the broader world. Going to law school in many ways connected with Betsy's long-standing interests.

At the same time, law school offered the possibility of new career directions—and the satisfaction of other values. It enabled her to develop a set of skills that she could rely on to make a solid income. Once she started working, she found that she enjoyed the precision and accountability of being a transactions lawyer. She also found lawyers and businesspeople capable, refreshingly down-to-earth, and, to her surprise, highly ethical. They were up-front about working for money and did what they said they would do. She had grown tired of people in the political world who claimed selfless motivations while working for their own advancement, or who were simply ineffective.

As her legal career developed, Betsy also found that she was part of the modern-day renaissance of China. As a corporate transactions lawyer, much of her work greases the wheels of capitalism. From her direct vantage point into China, she sees how the economic development of the past decades has significantly bettered the lives of hundreds of millions of people. She is glad to have had a constructive role in this.

Betsy's Tradeoffs

One of the reasons Betsy has been so successful in her legal career is that she has maintained a pretty clear sense of the tradeoffs involved in the job. There are parts of her career she likes a lot—having expertise, working with intelligent people, earning a lot of money, and living an international life, along with respect, stability, and a clear professional role. And there are parts that she doesn't particularly like—working extremely long hours, constant exhausting travel, being at the beck and call of clients at all hours, and being responsible for a huge number of things that are not under her direct control. Her work requires enormous investments of time and energy.

While the result appears glamorous and exciting, the story is more complex. Balance in the conventional sense is difficult. "In order to really perform at the very highest level," she says, "you have to have a level of dedication in and focus on your work that makes it very hard to have a personal life the way most people think about it."

Still, Betsy is happy with her career. It works. She knows her trade-offs and she is cool with them. She values certain aspects of her work very highly, especially the ability to be financially independent and the ability to deliver work consistent with her own standards of quality and ethics.

The Mystery of the Older Law Students

When I went to law school, a number of my classmates were a good ten or more years older than the average student—they were at least forty when they finished. Their backgrounds were quite different from one another, almost kookily so. They included an accountant, a priest, a music producer, several burned-out humanities professors, two or three doctors, a few engineers, a playwright, a failed entrepreneur, two Canadian art history professors, a Harvard MBA who had been working as a film critic, a physicist, and an economist.

Generally speaking, they were not especially involved in organizing clubs and did not really seek out leadership positions on the law review. They approached their studies seriously but not in a public, obsessive way. They were pleasant to be around, but did not leave a big footprint.

Yet, ten to fifteen years after graduation, almost every single one of these individuals is still practicing law, in marked contrast with many of their classmates. And most of them are content or happy with their careers.

I think there's a reason for this. These older students benefited from their previous life and work experience. Coming into law school, they knew there would be tradeoffs in practicing law, as there would be in any career. They did not start off expecting a career to be perfect, because experience had taught them that no career was likely to be perfect. They realized they would sometimes be in situations that they wouldn't particularly like and from which they could not easily escape. But they also expected that these negative things would be balanced by positive things. They were not concerned so much with particular problems as with how the overall mix balanced out.

Being Clear about What's Going On

Every career has tradeoffs. As in relationships, there are some people who settle for anything and others who are never satisfied with what they have because of the nagging feeling that somewhere out there is something better.

There are tradeoffs you can live with, and tradeoffs you can't. A huge part of personal development is figuring out which is which.

The ones you can live with are the normal b.s. that accompanies professional life. You wouldn't choose these things, but you can live with them. Part of the reason you can tolerate them is that you know you are likely to find similar issues in any other job. No job is b.s. free.

The tradeoffs you can't live with are things that violate your bottom line. They are problems that violate a core sense of who you are, deny the principles you live by, or poison the atmosphere you live in. When things violate your bottom line, you have to change the situation or get out of it. Note, however, that what violates one person's bottom line may not violate another's.

Career B.S.

Every career, no matter how wonderful, involves a certain amount of b.s. You will have to do things you don't want to do, deal with people you don't like, and be in situations you'd rather avoid. You could be a writer on a hit television series, a Montessori teacher, a concert violinist, the CEO of a socially responsible business, a Supreme Court justice, an entrepreneur, a poet, a warrior, a lifeguard, or a messiah—and you'd still have to deal with b.s.

I asked a number of people with interesting-sounding jobs what they found annoying or stressful about their professional worlds. Here is what they had to say.

Tenured college professor: "A large part of the job is grading papers, filling out administrative forms, attending faculty meetings, and working on unproductive committees. Since revenues to the institution depend on student enrollment, class size is often increased to reach budget. At the same time, there are pressures to cut expenses [copier use, etc.] because budgets have been exceeded. There are constant turf wars primarily arising from personal insecurities."

Fire chief: "It's extremely stressful to deal with the politics of the local government, including the very vocal neighborhood associations. There are numerous mandatory night meetings. Most of the meetings are exhausting and unproductive—we constantly rehash the same issues. Within the organization, management often falls back on a paramilitary

40

'because I said so' style. Decentralization creates a constant rumor mill that is not healthy for morale or effective for communications. While it is fulfilling to go on emergency calls as a firefighter, that is actually a small percentage of a firefighter's day."

Start-up consultant: "I do lots of chores related to business tracking: forecasting data, proposal data, time tracking, budget vs. actual-to-date figures, entering expense data, bookkeeping.... I have to think how everything I do ties to current or potential revenue. Some of my clients are not especially developed emotionally—they have low self-awareness, low empathy skills, and poor impulse control. Business travel is constant and decidedly unglamorous. It recently took me eleven hours to get from Palo Alto to Seattle, during which time I subsisted on pretzels and Diet Coke."

Investment manager: "The work is very document-intensive. For each company I follow, I have to review public filings like 10K, 10Q, 20F, 8K, 14DEF, 13F, 13G, 13D, Form 4, etc. I have to balance periods of deep research with networking. I would love just to do research, but to keep a roof over my head, I need to drive business. In the field of research-driven, value-oriented investing, the term *emotional intelligence* is unknown."

Assignments editor at a television network: "No matter how unique a story might be, the method of reporting it is exactly the same, every single time. There is a specific sequence of steps that have to be followed with zero room for flexibility. Additionally, you have to fill a certain number of hours of 'news' whether or not anything has actually happened. During holidays, you tear your hair out trying to figure out what you can put on when everyone else is just relaxing and enjoying themselves. The other situation is when there is actually a lot of significant news but you only have a fixed number of minutes to report it, so you end up leaving a lot out."

Physician specializing in infectious diseases and HIV treatment: "My job requires large amounts of boring and repetitive paperwork, especially for people applying for disability or Social Security benefits. In 90 percent of the cases, the people who ask me to fill out this paperwork are capable of working but don't seem to think they should have to. And while I'm proud that our clinic serves an underserved and indigent population, a large proportion of our demographic struggles with issues of substance abuse and criminal behavior. HIV medications have a substantial street value, as do prescription narcotics such as Percocet and Vicodin. Ethically, I am obliged to help someone who tells me he or she is suffering. But I am also obliged not to prescribe powerful narcotics to every Tom, Dick, and Harry who walks in the door. Navigating this is extremely stressful and exhausting."

B.S. You Can Live With

There are things that I don't like but that I can tolerate. I can make phone calls to strangers. I can work long hours. I can go without a title. I can listen to people cry. I can put up with financial strain. I can do boring things for fairly long periods of time. I can do my own QuickBooks. I can deal with skeptical or extremely low-energy audiences. I don't really *enjoy* these things, but I can put up with them provided they are not my entire job.

Exercise: B.S. You Can Live With

In the spaces below, describe the b.s. you can live with. Then circle those items that are frequent parts of your current job.

1. _____
2. _____
3. _____
4. _____
5. _____
6. _____
7. _____
8. _____
9. _____
10. _____

Violations of Your Bottom Line

When something violates your bottom line, we're not talking b.s. anymore. Instead, we're talking about things you cannot live with on any consistent basis. Maybe once or twice, but not consistently.

For example, I cannot deal with unethical people. I learned how important this was to me when, at a start-up company, I worked with an investor who turned out to be highly unethical.

Nor can I deal with jobs or situations that endanger my physical health or require long periods of time without regular sleep. Superficial as it might sound, I cannot work in really unattractive physical environments. Nor can I work in situations where I don't have frequent access to intelligent people.

I wouldn't say that I completely shut down in these situations, but they are fundamentally untenable. I would make huge sacrifices to avoid them, including leaving the job or career entirely.

Exercise: Identifying Your Bottom Line

In the spaces below, describe those things that violate your bottom line. Circle any of them that you are currently experiencing in your job.

1. _____
2. _____
3. _____
4. _____
5. _____

Identifying Tradeoffs

Knowing your tradeoffs involves being conscious of both the pluses and the minuses of a particular job or career. George, the junior associate doing structured finance, assessed some of them as follows:

Pluses	Minuses
• Good salary that goes up each year	• Long hours with occasional all-nighters
• Title and professional identity	• Colleagues complain a lot
• Everyone here is smart and informed on current events	• Limited time for outside interests
• Get free dinner when I work late	• Other people do not appear to share my ambitions

Exercise: Identifying Pluses and Minuses

List the pluses and minuses of your current situation, without judging which list outweighs the other.

Pluses	Minuses
• _____	• _____
• _____	• _____
• _____	• _____
• _____	• _____

Living with Ambivalence

Just because you make compromises doesn't mean something's wrong with your life. Life is full of unresolved issues, compromises, and trade-offs. Being clear about our tradeoffs is what frees us to go forward, without wasting energy on fighting reality. How we feel about these tradeoffs depends to a certain degree on how we describe them.

Consider how we express conflicting realities:

"I'm interested in venture capital, but I don't have the background or connections I need."

"I want a better life balance, but my clients are really demanding."

In each case, the *but* cancels out or at least minimizes the first part of the sentence so that the sentence weights toward the latter half. When you use *but*, you are unlikely to proceed with much energy. Things have been defined as an intractable problem. "I'm interested in venture capital, but I don't have the background or connections I need—*therefore there's no point in making the effort.*"

However, see what happens when you substitute *and* in the place of *but*:

"I'm interested in venture capital, *and* I don't have the background or connections I need."

"I want a better life balance, *and* my clients are really demanding."

Stated this way, the same realities offer new possibilities. You're stating a factual situation. Perhaps things will change and perhaps they won't, but the analysis isn't over yet. There might be creative solutions.

Exercise: The Power of "And"

Write a number of *and* statements that reflect some of the tradeoffs or ambivalences of your career. Try to come up with at least ten—this can be a very illuminating exercise.

Here are a few examples:

- The standards in my department are very high, *and* I do not have time to think through all the issues and prepare flawless work.
- I enjoy my colleagues, *and* they can be inappropriate and rude.
- I like international work, *and* I dislike spending time on airplanes.
- The attorneys working under me need a lot of support, *and* they do not realize how time-consuming their requests are.

Now write some of your own.

1. _____

_____

2. _____
_____

3. _____
_____

4. _____
_____

5. _____
_____

6. _____
_____

7. _____
_____

8. _____
_____

9. _____
_____

10. _____
_____

MP **Master Plan Intervention!**

Fill out the Tradeoffs and Bottom Line sections on the blank Master Plan template in the appendix.

Evaluation Point: What's Going On in Your Career?

Having reflected on the less appealing parts of your career, you are likely to have one of the following perspectives:

- Things are pretty great in my work.
- My work includes a certain amount of b.s., but no more than is to be expected.
- I spend more time than I like dealing with b.s., but my work does not violate my core values.
- Some of the aspects of my work life violate my core values. I need to take meaningful action to mitigate these.
- My work life is violating my core values in a fundamental and sustained way. I need to get out of this situation and find something better.

If any of the first three statements describes your current perspective, you are somewhere in the *normal world of employment*. Being satisfied is a question of optimizing what you have now and growing into what you'd like to become.

On the other hand, if either of the last two statements describes your current outlook, you are in a toxic situation. You need to make some changes. You might be able to cope with things, but this isn't where you should be spending your energy.

As we'll see in the following chapters, the tools for achieving small changes and large ones are basically the same.

ADDITIONAL EXERCISE: HOW MY JOB WORKS FOR ME

I once worked with a flight attendant named Antonia. At the time I met her, she had spent thirteen years working for a major airline and was bursting to do something else. What she wanted to do was write screenplays, get work doing voice-overs, and in general move into the creative life that she had downplayed in her first decades. For various reasons, primarily financial, she needed to continue working in her existing job, even though it paid far less than it used to as a result of successive collective bargaining give-backs. Her hours were unpredictable and erratic, and she was frustrated. But she wasn't ready to make a switch.

Antonia was in a tricky situation, one that I know well: it's when you don't like your life, but know you're going to be in it for a while.

One way to change this dynamic is to reexamine how you are looking at life, to see if there's a perspective that makes you happier and stronger. I asked Antonia to write an essay on the topic: "How My Job Works for Me." This is what she wrote:

> As a flight attendant with a major carrier, I have a flexible work schedule with flight benefits. My job has allowed me the opportunity to chat with former presidents, foreign dignitaries, and high-profile celebrities. I've received invitations from all kinds of new acquaintances, running the gamut from prime ministers to musicians. Being a flight attendant has opened worlds to me that I might otherwise not step into, and it has brought me some great resources for my personal development.
>
> For example, some years back I was having trouble with two of my college courses: Appreciation of Art and Music and Introduction to Acting.
>
> In music class, I could hear but could not clearly define some of the differences among melody, rhythm, and beat. Little did I know

that the gentleman on my flight enjoying his music was Ric Ocasek of The Cars. During our conversation, he was able to clear up my confusion on these topics as well as define other aspects of composition. I passed the course with an A.

Delivering my lines in acting class was challenging, until actor Alec Baldwin spent time in flight directing me on how to connect with my character and the best ways to incorporate props. My professor noticed my improvement at the very next class.

When I became interested in directing movies, Stan Dragoti, the director of *Necessary Roughness*, *Mr. Mom*, and *Love at First Bite*, set up a meeting for me in New York to help me map out the necessary steps to take in order to become a director. I also met director John Duigan, who at the time was shooting *Molly*, staring Elizabeth Shue, in Los Angeles. He invited me to observe the action on a working set and spent time explaining how and why he chose to set up shots in a particular way.

And it was on a flight from San Francisco to New York that I met my coach, a smiling, intelligent young man who chatted with me while stretching his legs in the back of the plane. It was the first of many conversations, in-person at first and then by phone and email when I was sent to Afghanistan as an Army Reservist. And it was my job that allowed us to show up in each other's lives.

Exercise: "How My Job Works for Me"

Take twenty minutes to write a short essay, "How My Job Works for Me."

READING LIST

Being clear about your professional tradeoffs is related to the broader idea that the perspectives you create about your life strongly influence how satisfied you are with it. The follow books explore this theme in compelling ways.

Benjamin and Rosamund Zander, *The Art of Possibility*

Benjamin Zander is the conductor of the Boston Philharmonic. Rosamund Zander, his wife, is an executive coach. Together, they draw lessons from the experiences of musicians and apply them to the world of work and life in general. A beautiful, smooth read. Great when you're in the doldrums or out of ideas.

Srikumar S. Rao, *Are You Ready to Succeed?*

For more than a decade, Rao has taught a popular course at Columbia Business School on work/life satisfaction. This book contains its core messages and exercises. The book asserts that happiness and fulfillment are more likely to come from changes in your own perspectives and mental beliefs than by adopting specific achievement-based goals. (Or, to put it another way, if you don't have the right perspectives and beliefs, you won't be happy no matter what you achieve.)

Martin Seligman, *Authentic Happiness*

Seligman, an academic who focuses on positive psychology, attained renown for his book *Learned Optimism*. In *Authentic Happiness*, he reviews the theories and research behind how happiness works and comes up with specific, workable recommendations on how to increase yours.

www.happiness-project.com

Gretchen Rubin, a writer who was the editor of the *Yale Law Journal*, spent a year test-driving every theory on happiness she could find, from Aristotle to Oprah. Her blog, "The Happiness Project," is an intelligent, earnest report from the trenches of how to be happy.

CHAPTER 6

Exercising Vision

Our culture is ambivalent about vision. We talk a good game about strategy, planning, and farsightedness. Yet at the same time, we place a premium on being realistic and practical.

In the professional world, vision language is encouraged, provided it has a practical ring to it. People are encouraged to become highly effective people, to make themselves into millionaires next door, to enter the zone. These are decent goals, but they are limited. There's a lot more to vision than trying to become wealthy, respected, and physically fit.

Vision speaks to the soul. I have one life—what do I want to do with it? I am here now—where do I want to be in the future? Here's what I know—what would I like to learn?

Vision cannot be decoupled from strategy. A vision without an implementing strategy starts out pristine and enticing, but gradually becomes tattered and unconvincing. Put together, vision and strategy are powerful.

Although this chapter is entitled "Exercising Vision," it is more accurate to say that our subject is *envisioning*—the verb form is a truer expression than the noun. Vision is a muscle: the more you use it, the stronger you get. You develop comfort, range, and power.

Creating Career Visions

A great way to develop visions of the future is to write. Writing helps to flesh out existing ideas and also helps to develop new ideas when your mind feels blank.

When clients tell me they don't know what they want to do with their lives, I usually find that, in fact, they want to do many things. They just don't know how to choose from a number of vague alternatives or how to figure out if these alternatives represent anything real. So the first step is to try to get a clearer sense of what we're considering, by fleshing out these potential alternatives. Oddly, while trying to think of one great vision statement can be quite difficult, thinking of *several* vision statements is not so hard. And the more vision statements you write, the easier it is to see which ones are truly compelling.

Let me give you a few examples. You'll notice that each of these features a mixture of work and life, and that they are written in the present tense.

- I'm a social entrepreneur. I run an innovative, cool organization that helps poor people in the Third World move ahead in their lives. Although the work is based overseas (mostly in southern Africa), I still live in the United States. My job is to do strategy, fundraising, and operations for the organization. I use my corporate legal training to keep the organization efficient and compliant with regulations. I frequently visit our projects overseas. The work involves lots of kids and teenagers, so there is constant positive energy, which I love.
- I am working in real estate transactions, but now work on the project-development side rather than the bank-financing side. I get to be involved in developing interesting projects from beginning to end rather than just transacting deals. On the weekends, my husband and I drive around North Carolina looking at organic farms to invest in and eating lots of great food.
- I am a full-time parent, having stopped working to be with my kids during their early years. I'm there for their first steps, words, and friends. I do creative projects at their ethnically diverse school, drawing on my professional skills and network. I also maintain my professional skills and connections by serving as a legal resource to the school community: I'm the go-to person for the parent association on legal matters, I help the school's trustees negotiate agreements with contractors, and I am writing position papers for a friend who is running for the school board.
- I am a partner at the firm where I began as an associate ten years ago. I'm putting my imprimatur on our personnel and assignment policies. Because of my efforts, my firm is now widely recognized as a good place to work. I maintain work/life balance by staying physically fit and teaching a class to recent immigrants on political involvement.

Exercise: Creating Career Vision Statements

As a first step, make a quick list of everything you might possibly do—anywhere from three to ten years in the future—whether these possibilities exist inside or outside of the practice of law. You can describe full-time positions or things that you might do as part of, or in addition to, your primary job. Be imaginative.

Examples:

1. Work in China.
2. Become an assistant U.S. attorney.
3. Study interior design.
4. Start a cool nonprofit organization.
5. Do part-time real estate investment.
6. Become an adjunct law professor.
7. Become certified as a Pilates instructor.

Your career vision possibilities:

1. _____
2. _____
3. _____
4. _____
5. _____
6. _____
7. _____
8. _____
9. _____
10. _____

Now, pick three or four of these options to flesh out further. For each of these, write a short paragraph in the present tense, describing what your life is like when you are engaged in these things. The following questions may stimulate your imagination:

- What is your job called?
- What's great about it?
- What institutions or people do you work with?
- What fills your days?
- Where do you live?
- How do your existing skills transfer?
- What's hard or challenging?
- How are your work and life integrated?

Remember, your visions don't have to be realistic. Envisioning works by deepening and expanding your sense of what you want. We'll deal with reality later.

If helpful, use the prompts in table 6-1 to enrich your description, thinking about the extent to which you want these elements present in your vision.

Career Vision Statement #1

_____

_____

_____

_____

_____

_____

_____

_____

Career Vision Statement #2

_____

_____

_____

_____

_____

_____

_____

_____

Career Vision Statement #3

_____

_____

_____

_____

_____

_____

_____

_____

TABLE 6-1. ASPECTS OF PROFESSIONAL VISION			
Location	• Big city • Small or medium city • Suburbs • Rural • International	**Types of activities**	• Focused • Diverse • Regular • Always changing
Hours	• Extreme • Intense • 9-to-5 • Part-time	**Travel**	• A lot • Some • None
Interactivity	• Work constantly with others • Mixture of group and solo • Primarily alone	**Management**	• Oversee others • Team environment • Autonomous
Ways to interact with others	• Leading • Managing • Mentoring • Counseling • Supporting • Advising	**Sector**	• Company/firm • Governmental • Nonprofit • Entrepreneurial • Freelance
Field	• Law • Relevant to law but not practicing • Outside legal profession	**Degree of change**	• New occupation • Same occupation, different focus • Substantially similar
Other interests	• Creative • Athletic • Community • Political • Spiritual • Outdoors	**Family/ friends**	• Partnered or married • Single • Children/ no children • Extended family • Close friends • Pets

MP

Master Plan Intervention!

Copy one of your vision statements over to the blank Master Plan template in the appendix.

Exercise: Additional Vision Research—Doing Market Research on Yourself

If you have a conversation with a friend or colleague about your interests, goals, or possibilities, you'll get a certain amount of useful information. But if you create a short questionnaire and ask the same person specific questions (as a journalist or poll-taker would), you'll get much better advice. People respond well to formalized questioning. They just do.

I first used this exercise when I contemplated going into coaching. I wanted to make sure I wasn't idealizing this new career. I decided to collect data from people who knew me. Some of these were business colleagues, some were friends, one was my mom. I was amazed at how well people identified my talents and "issues." And I was impressed by the quality of their suggestions. People don't have to be experts at your job to be pretty knowledgeable about *you*.

Create a questionnaire and interview between five and eight people. I'd recommend six to ten questions, maximum. You might use some of the following prompts:

1. What are three things I do really well?

2. What are three things that I don't do as well?

3. Of the various jobs or experiences I've had, which ones have been the most "me"? Why?

4. What things do I get most excited about?

5. What things haven't I tried professionally that I would be good at?

6. How do I limit myself or get in the way of my own success?

7. Going forward, what types of things do you see me doing professionally?

8. What types of things do you *not* see me doing?

9. What are some lessons that I keep learning?

Exercise: Bypassing Your Inner Editor

Another good exercise is to interview yourself. Using a tape recorder, ask and answer the following questions:

1. What do you want out of your career?

2. What have you accomplished so far?

3. What do you still want to accomplish?

4. What resources does your career offer you right now?

5. How would you like to grow?

6. What's a goal you've put off for a long time?

7. What's a goal you're no longer interested in?

8. What's something you're interested in that you could do right now?

9. In what ways are you your own worst enemy?

10. In what ways are you your best friend?

Supporting Your Vision

One of the best things you can do for your career is to create a personal board of directors. This is a collection of people who know you, are interested in your well-being, and have useful points of view. You consult with them on a regular basis.

A person doesn't have to be famous, influential, or even successful to be a good board member. All that's required is knowledge in a particular area. Your sister will probably offer better insight than the head of the bar association.

What's in it for the other person? A lot more than you might think. When you ask individuals to be on your personal board of directors, you are showing a great deal of respect for them. It means you value their opinions and take their thoughts seriously. When you make regular connections, you have a real relationship rather than a transactional one. They are an important part of your life.

Exercise: Brainstorming Your Board

Write the name of someone you know who:

1. Is incredibly organized _____
2. Knows how to have fun _____
3. Knows everyone _____
4. Can give you encouragement in tough times _____
5. Can talk to you straight about your weaknesses _____
6. Is unfailingly logical _____
7. Is deeply empathetic _____
8. Is spiritually advanced _____
9. Can handle a crisis _____
10. Has known you since childhood _____
11. Is politically connected _____
12. Is entrepreneurial _____
13. Is good at raising kids _____
14. Is an expert on money _____
15. Is an expert on relationships _____
16. Is an expert on health _____
17. Is an expert at work/life balance _____
18. Is an expert in the type of work you do _____
19. Is an expert in a type of work that interests you _____

20. Gives good advice about office politics _____

21. Gives good advice about professional development _____

22. Gives good advice about how to get ahead _____

23. Thinks you are great at what you do _____

24. Thinks you have great talents other than law _____

25. Thinks you are a great person _____

List other potential nominees, and their area of contribution to your life:

1. _____

2. _____

3. _____

4. _____

5. _____

6. _____

Review the names you've written. Circle between six and ten names to be on your personal board of directors.

In the next two weeks, establish contact with each of these folks. One by one, at a pace that feels comfortable, update them on your life. Start filling them in on your vision. Make a habit of speaking with them. Incorporate them into your world.

MP

Master Plan Intervention!

List the names of your personal Board of Directors on the blank Master Plan template in the appendix.

How Visions Reshape Themselves

Visions morph. Like Buddhist deities, they may "manifest" in a variety of forms. Your true calling might be the first version of your vision, or it could be something that emerges several incarnations later.

When Carlo envisioned his ideal life, he saw himself as a forest ranger. He loved nature, loved experiencing life through his hands, loved life outside of cities and towns. However, Carlo was not a forest ranger. Carlo was a Yale law school graduate working as a senior associate for a large national firm in Manhattan. He spent his life shifting between his small office and his small apartment. He regularly worked successive all-nighters; his wife would come to visit him at midnight for a snack before returning home to their apartment alone. He was out of shape. His marriage was suffering. He knew objectively that this was not the life he wanted.

In a workshop that Carlo attended, one of the other participants said, "He's such a good guy. But I know he'll never quit his job. He certainly won't become a forest ranger. He'll keep doing this until he collapses."

Well, Carlo's colleague was right in one respect: He did not become a forest ranger. But she was wrong in another respect: He did change his life.

A year or so after he took the workshop, Carlo quit his job at the big firm to become associate general counsel for a major corporation head-quartered in South Carolina. He and his wife moved down south, bought a home with plenty of acreage, and completely changed their way of living.

His life is filled with legal work, and it's also filled with intimacy, time at home, and exploration of the natural world. He gets to be smart, well-paid, and respected, and he also gets to be himself.

This type of reshaping happens a lot.

Exercise: Interim Vision Assessment

How do you feel about the visions you've created? If none of them is compelling, revisit this exercise after going through the rest of the book. But if at least one is reasonably compelling, answer the following questions:

1. How closely does your life resemble this vision now?

2. How long might it take you to achieve this vision? What will you do in the meantime?

3. What new learning do you have to do to achieve it?

4. How are you communicating this vision?

5. How does your network need to grow or change?

We will investigate these topics in the chapters that follow.

Additional Examples of Career Vision Statements

- I've retired from my official legal career and have moved into my next stage. I'm deeply engaged in two things: working on my garden (and becoming a credible, self-taught horticulturalist in the process) and volunteering at a legal clinic run by my church. After thirty years doing business transactions, it's thrilling to figure out how to solve the problems that real people face.
- I'm a scriptwriter for the latest Aaron Sorkin legal dramedy. I develop plotlines and do initial versions of scripts for the season (I'm not responsible for rewrites or last-minute changes). I've honed my skills by taking classes in scriptwriting. Most of the people I work with are younger than me; they're neurotic and have good senses of humor. I have houses in both New York and Los Angeles.
- I'm an adjunct professor at a local law school. I really enjoy teaching students and not having to worry about publishing-or-perishing. For money, I continue practicing insurance defense. I am not sure what my long, long-term goal is, but I have a great platform for figuring that out.
- I work for the state government as a staff attorney for a key state representative. I got this job by gradually becoming involved in political campaigns at the local and then state level. When my candidate won, I was brought onto the team. I'm much appreciated for organizing a volleyball league where each team is balanced in terms of Republicans and Democrats.
- I own and operate a small retail store that stocks unique goods from around the world. I have strong relationships with my customers and coworkers. I do a variety of tasks all day rather than the same-old, same-old. I apply my creativity and business knowledge to something that I care about.

CHAPTER 7

Self-Management and Type

Let's take a quick quiz. Below are some short descriptions of different characteristics of law practice. For each one, check whether you find it appealing, have no strong opinion, or find it unappealing.

Quiz Time!

1. A logical system based on impersonal principles

Law is a system based on impersonal, neutral principles, just like accounting, finance, and science. Logic prevails over feeling. Law isn't people-based like social work, nor is it imagination-based like advertising.

    a. _____ This is appealing to me.
    b. _____ No strong opinion.
    c. _____ This is unappealing to me.

2. Abstract

Law deals with what-ifs. The work of many lawyers focuses on avoiding future problems. Legal analysis examines how particular situations logically relate to past situations as well as future, unknowable situations.

    a. _____ This is appealing to me.
    b. _____ No strong opinion.
    c. _____ This is unappealing to me.

3. Based on fact and precedent

Although there is a place for creativity within law, it is squarely grounded in a system that operates by examining facts and precedent. Law practice focuses on what *is* rather than what *should be*.

a. ____ This is appealing to me.
b. ____ No strong opinion.
c. ____ This is unappealing to me.

4. Detail-oriented

While law is a system of abstraction, it is grounded in detail and precision. Specific facts matter. So do specific holdings, specific contract provisions, and specific ways of phrasing things. All the *i*'s must be dotted and *t*'s crossed.

a. ____ This is appealing to me.
b. ____ No strong opinion.
c. ____ This is unappealing to me.

5. Requiring introverted behaviors

Law requires introverted behaviors. Lawyers often spend long periods of time studying, researching, writing, and thinking, especially in the early years of their careers.

a. ____ This is appealing to me.
b. ____ No strong opinion.
c. ____ This is unappealing to me.

6. Requiring extroverted behaviors

Law also requires extroverted behaviors. Lawyers often spend time attending meetings, managing subordinates and colleagues, attending judicial proceedings, counseling clients, and marketing their business. Generally speaking, the more senior you are, the more extroverted you will have to be.

a. ____ This is appealing to me.
b. ____ No strong opinion.
c. ____ This is unappealing to me.

7. Client-focused

Law is a service industry. Part of competing effectively is giving good client service, which means being seen as highly responsive to client points of view and, in particular, to client deadlines.

a. ____ This is appealing to me.
b. ____ No strong opinion.
c. ____ This is unappealing to me.

8. High personal stakes

Many clients face very high personal stakes. They are dealing with uncertain matters that may affect their wealth, business prospects, reputation, personal relationships, health, freedom, and, in certain cases, life and death.

    a. _____ This is appealing to me.
    b. _____ No strong opinion.
    c. _____ This is unappealing to me.

9. Long entry period and steep learning curve

Law is an apprenticeship field. Experienced lawyers say that it took anywhere from five to ten years before they started feeling that they knew what they were doing. People expect you to pay your dues and learn by doing, usually at the feet of people who are more senior.

    a. _____ This is appealing to me.
    b. _____ No strong opinion.
    c. _____ This is unappealing to me.

10. Need to develop business

Senior lawyers at large firms, most lawyers at small firms, and all self-employed lawyers must bring in business. This means less time doing actual legal work and more time managing client relationships, marketing, and selling.

    a. _____ This is appealing to me.
    b. _____ No strong opinion.
    c. _____ This is unappealing to me.

11. Adversarial aspects

Criminal law and civil litigation are fundamentally adversarial. Other types of law, particularly transactional, are not adversarial by nature although the people involved may make it seem that way.

    a. _____ This is appealing to me.
    b. _____ No strong opinion.
    c. _____ This is unappealing to me.

The answer to each of these questions is probably obvious to you. However, other lawyers would not necessarily answer the same way.

People have significantly different preferences about how they like to work, even when they are in the same profession or have the same job. While we may recognize this in theory, we tend to act otherwise: If we enjoy something, we tend to assume that other normal, good people will enjoy it as well; if we find something unpleasant or distasteful, we presume that others will, too.

In fact, people who have very similar values may nonetheless have quite different work-style preferences. For example, Mark and Susan, two individuals who share a strong desire to make a social contribution, might answer questions 2 and 3 above differently. Mark, an idealistic person who enjoys broad-brush, abstract thinking, would probably enjoy impact litigation. In contrast, Susan, an idealistic person who is highly focused on the world of real, practical experience, may feel that such work is too detached from actual people and results to be meaningful. Why are we talking about lofty constitutional principles, Susan asks, when there are homeless people on the streets outside our office? She might find the constant client service and problem-solving inherent in immigration work to be very satisfying. But Mark might end up getting bored by the repetition of such work. How much impact can we have working on just a handful of cases, he muses, when the laws themselves need to be reformed?

Work satisfaction depends significantly on *how* we actually work, not just on *what* we are working *toward*. It's easy to assume that if we are working for a goal we consider important—whether that's changing the world or making tons of money—that we will enjoy the work we do. However, *this is not necessarily true*.

If you understand your own preferences for *how* you like to work, you will illuminate a major part of the mystery about how you can achieve professional satisfaction. Using "type" is a great way to do this.

The Insight of Type

When I was in law school, a popular belief was that law students were of two kinds: the public-interest type and the corporate type. Most students believed this, and many law professors, who generally had very little work experience outside of teaching law, believed it, too.

According to this categorization, life after law school would follow one of two simple narratives: you would pursue public-interest law and live poor and happy, or you would go into corporate work and make a lot of money.

Obviously, this was not a robust categorization. There are many paths out of law school, and the many individuals who comprised my law school class could not be confined to these two categories. The people I went to school with were individuals, with all kinds of differences in personality, interests, values, and style. They would approach their careers from different points of view.

The type of job you have does not say much about your personality. However, your personality may say a fair amount about the type of situation you prefer to be in and the ways you prefer to work. *Type theory* is one way to look at personality differences and how they show up in careers.

Type theory is based on the work of Swiss psychologist Carl Jung and was elaborated over a period of several decades by two women, Katharine Cook Briggs and her daughter Isabel Briggs Myers. Type is assessed by a questionnaire called the Myers-Briggs Type Indicator, or MBTI.[1] For more than fifty years, individuals, companies, governments, and academic institutions have used the MBTI for training, counseling, performance improvement, and team-building. Since 1962, more than four thousand research studies have been conducted on the use of the MBTI. Currently there are more than two million administrations of the instrument each year. It's a solid tool.

Type assesses preferences for four sets of alternatives that describe an individual's mental processes: extroversion/introversion, sensing/intuition, thinking/feeling, and perceiving/judging. According to the theory, we have the capacity to access all of these functions but we prefer certain ones over others, much as the vast majority of people favor one hand over the other when writing.

Extroversion and *introversion* relate to where energy flows. Extroverts are energized by the external world, people, and activities. Introverts are energized by the inner world of ideas and feelings, as well as their own space. Questions 5, 6, 7, and 10 (introverted behaviors, extroverted behaviors, client-focused, need to develop business) loosely relate to the extroversion/introversion dichotomy.

Sensing and *intuition* refer to how individuals perceive the external world. Sensing types notice facts and concrete reality. They trust experience. Intuitive types notice ideas, patterns, and possibilities. They like newness for its own sake. Questions 2, 3, 4, and 9 (abstract, based on fact and precedent, detail-oriented, long entry period and steep learning curve) loosely relate to the sensing/intuition dichotomy.

Thinking and *feeling* refer to how we assess information and make decisions. They are both methods of thinking. Thinking types prefer to make decisions based on logic and objective, impartial principles.

---

[1]"Myers-Briggs Type Indicator" and MBTI are registered trademarks of the Myers-Briggs Type Indicator Trust in the United States and other countries.

Feeling types prefer to make decisions based on subjective values and how actions affect other people. Questions 1, 7, 8, 10, and 11 (logical system, client-focused, high-stakes, need to develop business, adversarial aspects) loosely relate to the thinking/feeling dichotomy.

Perceiving and *judging* refer to attitudes toward closure. Perceiving types feel freedom in keeping things open. They prefer spontaneity. Judging types feel freedom in making decisions. They prefer having things scheduled. Questions 4, 7, and 9 (detail-oriented, client-focused, long entry period and steep learning curve) loosely relate to the perceiving/judging dichotomy.

Type theory is based on the idea that people are different in ways that are at least partly predictable. Type can shed a great deal of light on the process of how to be satisfied in work. It won't tell you what to do with your life, but it will identify some challenges you are likely to face and point to strategies for dealing with them, as well as highlighting activities you naturally enjoy.

How Preferences Play Out in Work

The best way to assess type is to take the MBTI itself, whether in the workplace or through an independent administrator. There are also numerous excellent books that clearly explain and apply the MBTI. Some of these are listed at the end of the chapter. However, we can summarize some of the principal aspects of type as they relate to the work lawyers do.

As you read each description, note whether it sounds like you. Where both sound like you to a degree, highlight the elements that seem most relevant.

Extroversion and Introversion

Extroverts are energized by people, activities, and the external world (see table 7-1). Extroverts enjoy interacting with people in the course of business. They are comfortable at meetings and find it easy to talk to strangers. They think out loud, enjoy running ideas past others, and like to brainstorm. Extroverts like variety and getting out of the office. A lawyer with a preference for extroversion will be happiest in environments and practice areas where she can be vocal, interact with others, and not be tied to a desk. Extroverts who spend long periods of time alone wilt if they don't get recharged through some kind of extroverted activity.

Introverts are energized by the inner world of ideas and feelings. They enjoy time alone and need their own space. Introverts think before they speak and speak only if they have something to say. Introverts generally

TABLE 7-1. EXTROVERSION VS. INTROVERSION		
	Favors Extroversion	**Favors Introversion**
School	• Large classes • Open discussion • Talking in class	• Self-study • Research and writing • Preparing for class
Communication	• Group • Variety • Meeting new people • In-person	• One-on-one • Established relation-ships • Email or other written • Phone
Work style	• Discuss first, then read • Meetings • Teams • Client interactions • Business development • Recruiting and interviewing	• Read first, then discuss • Research • Writing • Contemplation • Relationships based on meaningful work or interaction • Privacy

enjoy jobs that include periods of solitude where they have the opportunity to work things out on their own. An introvert will be happiest in environments and practice areas where he can hear himself think and have clear boundaries on his space and the demands others place on him. Introverts are less happy in situations that demand lots of face time, long hours spent in mandatory meetings, and superficial interactions with other people.

Sensing and Intuition

Sensing types trust facts, personal experience, and details (see table 7-2). They know it when they see it and like to see it before they believe it. Lawyers with a preference for sensing easily identify and remember details, whether they're facts in a case, bullet points on a PowerPoint presentation, or typos on a prospectus. They prefer concrete reality to grand theories and favor the tried and true over newfangled ideas. They usually want to figure things out themselves rather than move forward on the basis of other people's judgments.

TABLE 7-2. SENSING VS. INTUITION		
	Favors Sensing	**Favors Intuition**
School	• Probing into specific cases • Mastering precedent • Substantive and procedural classes	• Distinguishing cases • Tying together disparate theories • Policy and theoretical classes
Work strengths	• Knowledge of facts • Knowledge of case law and statutes • Keeping track of details • Realistic • Proofreading	• Grasping the main idea • Strategy • Telling a story • Scholarship • Setting priorities • Innovation
Practice areas	*All areas*, but may be happier in: • Real estate • Tax • General practice • Trusts & estates • Routine and/or code-based	*All areas*, but may be happier in: • Policy and impact litigation • Litigation • Labor law • Teaching • IP or other fast-changing fields

Sensing types enjoy legal work that is focused on specifics, details, realistic scenarios, and actual facts. They prefer to work in areas in which they have experience, rather than branching out endlessly into new areas. Aspects of legal work that appeal to sensing types are the precedential nature of work, the reliance on facts, and clear role-definitions. Sensing types sometimes run into trouble when it comes to seeing the big picture, setting priorities, or coming up with new methods of solving problems.

Intuitive types are interested in theory, new ideas, patterns, and possibilities. They enjoy thinking about the big picture, coming up with innovative ways to solve problems, and figuring out how things fit together. Intuitives often view law as a type of social science—it's a way to connect together different sets of social, political, and economic phenomena. Some intuitives are interested in law as a system; others are more interested in it as a tool for achieving other social or political objectives.

Law lends itself to the intuitive mindset, so, depending on their interests and values, intuitives may be drawn toward civil rights and constitutional practice, policy and government work, deal-making, scholarship, or other areas. Intuitives are not very interested in details. Tasks like proofreading, cite-checking, and coordinating scores of documents will not get their best energies. Intuitives may resist the strong conservative preference that law has for facts and precedent.

Thinking and Feeling

Thinking types prefer to reach conclusions and make decisions on the basis of impartial, objective principles (see table 7-3). They esteem logic. Justice, to a thinker, means doing what is fair according to neutral principles. Thinkers respect communication that is straight-shooting and clear. They want to be evaluated for what they do, as opposed to who they are. When counseling others, they try to maintain a neutral, detached perspective.

In many respects, law is a thinker's paradise, since it's a system based on logic and neutral principles. Thinkers are naturally attracted to those aspects of law that value logic and impartial analysis, ranging from litigation to transactional work, impact litigation, and legal scholarship. Thinkers are less comfortable where their success depends on their abilities to read and empathize with people (such as client development, personnel management, and close negotiations), where the situation calls for subjective or value judgments, or where they need to motivate others or deal with personal conflict.

Feeling types prefer to reach conclusions and make decisions on the basis of subjective factors—strongly held personal values or the effect of the decisions on other people. Justice, to a feeler, means doing right for a particular person or group. Feelers easily step into mentoring or counseling roles; they can be the glue that makes teams work. Feelers are sensitive to conflict and good at defusing it because of their ability to put themselves in the shoes of others.

Feelers are most fulfilled when they work closely with people they like or for an important cause, when they are able to express their thoughts and feelings openly, and where they feel appreciated. They are less comfortable working in tense or dispassionate environments, in situations where they are evaluated strictly by results or output, or when doing work for which they see no ultimate human benefit.

TABLE 7-3. THINKING VS. FEELING		
	Favors Thinking	*Favors Feeling*
School	• Logical analysis • Case study • Socratic method • Competition • Debate	• Values or policy analysis • Team work • Clinical work • Advocacy
Work functions	• All standard legal work • Strategy • Operations	• Client service • Team management • Counseling, mentoring, training, and development • Negotiations • Recruiting, marketing, and outreach • Pro bono
Practice areas	*Almost all fields*, including: • Litigation and transactional • Tax • Procedural • Bankruptcy • Criminal (prosecution and defense)	• Most types of advocacy • Criminal • Immigration • Family law • Environmental • Trusts & estates • Counseling/coaching

Judging and Perceiving

Individuals with a preference for **judging** are sometimes called "scheduling types." They feel a sense of freedom when they make decisions (see table 7-4). They are comfortable making plans, setting dates, and coming to decisions relatively quickly. They usually work before they play, and may rarely play.

Lawyers with a preference for judging will prefer work that is structured, organized, and of predictable hours. They want to work with people who stick to deadlines. Judging lawyers will be less comfortable in situations that involve hurry-up-and-wait scenarios, disorganized bosses or teams, or a strong process orientation. They particularly dislike

70

TABLE 7-4. PERCEIVING VS. JUDGING		
	Favors Perceiving	*Favors Judging*
Personal Style	• Spontaneous • Open-ended • Don't like being tied down • May find it difficult to buckle down and do routine tasks • Play before you work	• Scheduled • Organized • Don't like having too many things up in the air • May find it difficult to relax and have fun • Work before you play
Work style	• Variable productivity • "All or nothing" or "I only have one speed" • Make lists to make sure they don't forget crucial items • Able to process midstream change	• Consistent effort and productivity • Multitasking • Make lists because it's fun to make lists • Dislike midstream changes
Practice areas	*All fields.* May be more comfortable in: • Work in which spontaneity is valued (e.g., trial work) • Work in which there are a few big deadlines (e.g., litigation) rather than frequent, recurring deadlines • Work where going deep is valued more than getting it done quickly (e.g., tax, appellate, academia)	*All fields.* May be more comfortable in: • Work that is focused on a clear external goal (e.g., transactional, in-house, legislative) • Work where your abilities to organize and manage projects and teams are valued • Situations with rational and predictable schedules

having their own schedules determined by people who are less organized, responsible, or efficient than they are.

Individuals with a preference for **perceiving** are sometimes called "spontaneous" types. They like to keep things open, preferring to gather more information ("perceive" more) rather than making an unnecessarily hasty decision. Perceiving types get things done on time, but the process may involve a fair amount of unstructured rumination accompanied by a mad dash at the end. Strict schedules and forced decisions make perceiving types feel hemmed in. Once perceiving types do get involved in a project, they often have the ability to focus deeply until it's done to their satisfaction.

Lawyers with a preference for perceiving will enjoy jobs with enough structure to guide them but not so much as to burden them. They do best in situations where their preference for spontaneity will be valued, such as in dealing with last-minute changes, the introduction of new parties, or responding to compelling new information. Perceivers will be less happy in situations where their time is micromanaged, where there is a great detail of routine, or where they need to make even progress on several major projects at the same time.

The judging/perceiving dichotomy shows up mainly in personal relationships and work style, rather than indicating a preference for particular kinds of work.

Managing Your Energy and Working toward Balance

The extroversion/introversion preference relates to energy. Figuring out how to manage your energy effectively can make a huge contribution to your happiness and career success.

Exercise: Analyze Your Energy Flow

You are best off doing difficult things when you have the most energy, saving easier activities for low-energy times.

What's your energy flow like throughout the day? Briefly describe your high and low periods.

1. High period _____
2. High period _____

1. Low period _____

2. Low period _____

Of your work demands, what's relatively hard? What's relatively easy?

1. Harder _____

2. Harder _____

3. Harder _____

1. Easier _____

2. Easier _____

3. Easier _____

Experiment with doing your "hard" things during your period of maximum energy and reserving your "easy" things for low-energy periods. Fill in the blanks in the following paragraphs.

I typically have my highest energy at _____ and
_____. I will try using this time to do _____,
_____, and _____, activities
that are sometimes challenging for me.

I typically have my lowest energy at _____
and _____. Instead of depleting myself further with
tough things, I will instead try doing _____,
_____, and _____,
things that come pretty naturally to me.

Exercise: Raising Your Energy Levels by Building on Your Strengths

Good self-management includes building on tasks you do naturally, while not being limited by your natural preferences.

Depending on your preference for extroversion or introversion, fill out one of the following charts. Brainstorm ways that you can use your core preferences more effectively, and also stretch yourself past your comfort zone.

73

PREFERENCE FOR EXTROVERSION

Extroverted activities connect you with people, activities, and the external world.

Enhancing My Preference (Doing What I Like)	Not Being Limited by My Preference (Stretching Myself)
Examples	**Examples**

- Take part in more candidate interviews (especially if lunch is included!)
- Join firm personnel committee
- Join nighttime intramural sports league

- Put my thoughts into writing before I speak with introverted partners
- Do heavy legal writing early in the morning when there are fewer distractions
- Practice letting other people speak first

1. _____

2. _____

3. _____

4. _____

5. _____

1. _____

2. _____

3. _____

4. _____

5. _____

PREFERENCE FOR INTROVERSION

Introverted behaviors connect you with the inner world of ideas and feelings and your own space.

Enhancing My Preference (Doing What I Like)	Not Being Limited by My Preference (Stretching Myself)
Examples	**Examples**

- Get to work an hour earlier to have time to collect my thoughts

- Join a bar committee I'm interested in

- Volunteer for research project valued by my firm (e.g. standard forms project)
- Tell junior associates I can answer their questions more easily if they email them

- Go to a conference in my field
- Take course in public speaking

1. _____

_____

2. _____

_____

3. _____

_____

4. _____

_____

5. _____

_____

1. _____

_____

2. _____

_____

3. _____

_____

4. _____

_____

5. _____

_____

MP

Master Plan Intervention!

Fill out the "Self-Management—Manage my energy" section of the blank Master Plan template in the appendix.

Majority and Minority in the Field of Law

Whether you *feel* that you fit into your career (key word: *feel*) depends, in part, on how common your type is. If everyone seems like you, you fit in. If everyone seems different, you feel like you don't fit in.

Within the realm of type, certain preferences are dominant within the field of law. They have a significantly different distribution from the general U.S. population. Lawyers, as a whole, have clear preferences for introversion, intuition, and thinking. (The split for judging/perceiving in law is not much different from the overall U.S. population.) The most important of these, from the point of view of whether people feel they fit in, is the majority's preference for thinking.

The Thinking Majority

Consider the data in tables in this chapter, based on type surveys of 3,014 lawyers conducted in 1993 by Larry Richard, a lawyer and psychologist, compared with type surveys of the general population.

TABLE 7-5. THINKING/FEELING IN THE LEGAL COMMUNITY COMPARED TO THE GENERAL POPULATION		
	Thinking	*Feeling*
U.S. Population (male)	60%	40%
Legal Profession (male)	81%	19%
U.S. Population (female)	35%	65%
Legal Profession (female)	66%	34%

What do the data show? That law is overwhelmingly dominated by thinkers. Thinking perspectives are the default perspectives. They are the common vocabulary, the default line of inquiry, the majority vote. Thinkers are normal.

Feelers experience this dominance in two ways. First, feelers are regularly called on to use a manner of thinking that is not their innate preference. They can do so—anyone who has graduated from law school is capable of performing in a thinking way—but the work will generally be more draining for feelers than thinkers. Second, feelers are outnumbered, and this can lead to a perception, both by themselves and by their fellow lawyers, that they are not quite normal. Their natural responses, when expressed, may seem out of the ordinary and at times downright wacky. They will raise issues that other people have little interest in, do not value, and lack the skills to evaluate.

The dominance of thinking is not, however, an unalloyed benefit for thinkers. Homogeneity has its downsides. When you are good at a particular skill, you naturally favor it. But your weaknesses stay the same or worsen. A legal group comprised solely of thinkers may lack access to relevant feeling perspectives. But because of groupthink, which often happens in situations of high homogeneity, it might never occur to them that they are missing something.

What is the legal profession criticized for? Among other things, the field is taken to task for adversarial posturing, insensitivity, detachment, and treating clients and lawyers like objects. These are words that could describe a malignant version of thinking—thinking without the balance of feeling. Take the same words down a few notches, and adversarial posturing becomes commitment to principle, insensitivity becomes logic, detachment becomes fairness, and treating clients and lawyers like objects becomes neutrality.

Tips for Feelers	*Tips for Thinkers*
Find your own. Identify people with whom you feel immediately comfortable. These are probably other feelers. Make time for talking to and hanging out with them. Focus on positive topics.	***Ask how people will react.*** Once you have assessed situations or made tentative decisions, take time to think about and discuss how people will respond, and how these responses might change either what you decide or how you communicate it.
Build your relationships. Do what makes you feel good. Make friends. Train new lawyers. Mentor students. Plan birthday parties for your secretaries and colleagues.	***Practice active listening.*** Listen carefully, restate what the other person has said, and ask for clarification. Active listening is a way of valuing other people.
Share with the right people. Identify a couple of trusted people with whom you can share your difficult feelings. Ask if it's okay if you occasionally call them specifically for this. Don't vent with everyone.	***Show appreciation.*** Take time to show appreciation for *who people are* in addition to *what people do*.
Pretend you're a thinker. When you're stressed or confused, imagine you're Spock from *Star Trek*. Examine the situation logically. This really works—I'm a feeler myself.	***Check in on your own feelings.*** Make a habit of checking in with your own feelings. Ask whether you like or don't like how things are going.
Practice pretending others are feelers. When a thinker acts in a way that you interpret as cold, unsupportive, or distant, do a quick mental reinterpretation. *"If he were a feeler, rather than a thinker, he would probably smile and say how much he appreciates my being on the team. But he's a thinker, so that doesn't occur to him."*	***Weigh values.*** Incorporate values-based questions like, "What's the right thing to do?" "How do we like the results?" "Should we reexamine first principles?" "Is this consistent with our core values?"
	Signal when you need time to reflect. Thinkers typically think about their feelings before knowing clearly what they are. Signal when you need time to reflect. *"That's a really good question, and I need some time to think it over. Can I get back to you tomorrow morning?"*

Tips for Feelers	*Tips for Thinkers*
Admire thinkers (and the latent thinking part of you). Overrelying on the feeling preference limits your humanity. Observe thinkers in action. Admire logic, neutrality, and distance. Think about the ways that these qualities help people.	*Take breaks after emotionally laden situations.* Situations that are highly intimate, where there is heightened emotion (like crying), or where you have to make decisions based on subjective factors may be exhausting. Know your limits and take breaks.

The Introvert Paradise

In the U.S. population as a whole, extroverts outnumber introverts three to one. Our culture values extroversion to the point where many people feel uncomfortable being described as "introverted"—they think it's bad. Introverts are forced to learn to manage the demands of an extroverted world. Introverts who succeed in the business world often figure out how to feign extroversion.

The field of law is a different world, however. The majority of lawyers are introverts, as shown in table 7-6.

Introvert characteristics are more apt to be accepted and appreciated in the field of law than in the rest of the world. Introvert-dominant environments are likely to place a value on quiet, privacy, reading, writing skills, working alone, extended contemplation, careful preparation, thinking before speaking, getting to know people before warming up, and email or telephone communication as opposed to face-to-face meetings.

Extroverts, who usually go through life without consciously reflecting on their style, may sometimes feel like outsiders in the legal world. (This depends greatly on the particular practice area or microenvironment they are in.) Their energy, enthusiasm, and words are not necessarily welcomed. Introverted bosses will not have a great deal of patience for chatty subordinates or for those who prefer thinking out loud. For

TABLE 7-6. *EXTROVERSION/INTROVERSION IN THE LEGAL COMMUNITY COMPARED TO THE GENERAL POPULATION*

	Extroversion	Introversion
U.S. Population	75%	25%
Legal Profession	43%	57%

TABLE 7-7. SENSING/INTUITION IN THE LEGAL COMMUNITY COMPARED TO THE GENERAL POPULATION

	Sensing	Intuition
U.S. Population	70%	30%
Legal Profession	30%	70%

their part, extroverts may misconstrue the quietness and containment of their colleagues as aloofness.

Law requires both introverted *and* extroverted functions, so both introverts and extroverts need to make adaptations. The previous exercises on managing your energy are good ways to think about how to make these adaptations.

Sensing/Intuition

Just as law is dominated by thinkers, so is it dominated by intuitive types (see table 7-7).

The sensing/intuition preference does not seem to play out in feelings of "belonging" or "not belonging" as much as the thinking/feeling preference. Law requires both intuition and sensing at all levels—you have to get both the theory *and* the facts, the main idea *and* the details. For every lawyer, some aspects are natural and others a bit more draining.

Tips for Sensors	Tips for Intuitives
Do research about real-world jobs. Sensors are likely to be significantly happier in legal jobs that feel "real." Investigate alternatives. *Figure out your priorities and rank them in terms of value.* Sensing types sometimes treat all tasks as equally important. Rank your priorities—it will make it easier to give up the lower-value things.	*Accept that you must get details right.* There's really no way around it: in law, you have to get the details right. This means typo-free documents, correct case cites, procedures followed exactly, and all the documents in the closing having been set up correctly.

Tips for Sensors	*Tips for Intuitives*
Ask for help on the big picture. Sensing types are often beloved as subordinates because they get everything done. However, as they try to ascend to senior levels, they are sometimes tossed aside because they are perceived as not getting the big picture. If this is a weak point for you, find mentors or colleagues who will support your continued learning in this area.	**Develop resources to help you on details and execution.** I knew a midlevel attorney who arranged for colleagues at his firm to proofread his work before submitting it to partners. This was a great solution. It also is suggestive of a larger point: it's crucial for intuitives to have strong support staff. This means putting in the time and effort to build your team, ranging from attorneys to mailroom employees. Help them rise to the level of competence you want with training, support, and constructive feedback.
Practice giving feedback in summary form. When giving feedback, rather than jumping in and going point by point, start out with an overview. *"The three things I most like about this brief are (a), (b), and (c). The three ways I'd like you to improve it are (d), (e), and (f)."*	**Rank-order your priorities.** Intuitives typically have lots of plans, most of which will take far more time and resources than they realize. Be clear about what your priorities actually are so you don't get distracted.
Encourage intuitive colleagues to flesh out their visions before you identify flaws. Let your intuitive colleagues fully explain their thoughts before you raise issues, especially if you are in a supervisory role. Ask lots of questions that start with *what* ("What else would be good about this?") or *how* ("How do you see this developing?").	**Come down from 30,000 feet.** To work effectively with colleagues and clients, make sure that you incorporate discussion of practicalities and logistics.
Pick new topics to learn about. Stretch yourself by identifying new things to learn about. Make a habit of occasionally trying new things just for the sake of newness.	**Identify friends to brainstorm with.** Intuitives live for thinking and expressing ideas. Spend time each day with friends or colleagues talking about ideas, regardless of the other pressures on you.

Managing Yourself Creatively

Does all this mean that nondominant types should get out of the field?
No.

The value of type is showing ways to manage yourself and understand others. Type is a useful antidote to the somewhat poisonous tendencies we have to expect other people to be just like us, and to think that if they aren't, something is either wrong with them or wrong with us.

People are different. They will get juiced up or drained by different things.

Exercise: How Do Things Fit?

How does your type fit your job? And what can you do to manage the fit?

Write out answers to the following questions.

1. To what extent does your type fit your job?

2. To what extent does your type not fit your job?

3. What can you do to improve things?

Box 7-1. Example: How Do Things Fit?

Jane, the lawyer from chapter 1 who now works as the executive director of a regional nonprofit, assessed her type/job match as follows.)

To what extent does your type fit your job?
I'm definitely a feeler. When I was in-house counsel at the bank, I would express this by having good relationships with my colleagues. Now I express it by working on behalf of a cause that I believe in.

To what extent does your type not fit your job?
As an introvert, I'm not crazy about networking on behalf of my organization, hobnobbing with the staff and board, and—God forbid—making cold calls to potential donors. However, I need to do these things to be effective. I don't have the same relationships with my staff that I did with my colleagues at the bank.

What can you do to improve things?
I can make more time for interacting with my former colleagues, as well as with other intelligent lawyers or nonprofit directors. I think I would benefit from studying "best practices" for approaching and managing donors. If I took a class or worked with a consultant, I would feel more confident and then would find the whole process less off-putting.

The Value of Differences

You don't have to be part of the mainstream to enjoy or be successful at your work. If you are in the minority, you may face additional challenges, but you also have something unique to offer.

Jacob Froh is a feeler who works for a large international law firm, following stints as a Ph.D. candidate and in other jobs. While he can turn on logical thinking when he needs to, he believes that his natural inclination is to think more associatively—like a feeler. But being surrounded by thinkers works for him.

"I like being in a thinking environment," Jacob says, "because I've seen the extreme alternative. When I was a graduate student in English, the feeling perspective ruled to the exclusion of all else. People were evaluated by subjective standards only. You were either 'interesting' or you weren't, and you never had any idea how professors were making these evaluations. Once you were labeled, there was no escape. It was a horrible dystopia.

"I *like* being in an institution where I'm judged according to objective criteria. I can see what I'm dealing with here."

Chris Palamountain is another feeler, a very extroverted one. When you meet her, the phrase "people person" comes to mind. I asked if she thought that feelers were less comfortable practicing law.

"Actually," she replied, "I think that's my strength. I can reach across barriers and establish relationships with people."

In fact, she sees difficult people as interesting challenges.

"When I deal with real jerks, I see it as a challenge to find some way to connect with them. And I usually can. It's interesting, and very fulfilling, to see what I can accomplish basically just by being nice. It's made me much more successful."

Type is a way to manage yourself and understand others. Once you figure out your own needs, you can focus on finding ways to fulfill them. At that point, you can make a contribution based on strength.

READING LIST

The MBTI

You can take the MBTI through a variety of accredited ("qualified" in the official lingo) sources that you can easily find on the Web. Just type "Myers Briggs Type Indicator" or "take MBTI" in the search box. (A number of websites provide quick-and-dirty free versions of the instrument, but these are not backed by any actual research.)

There are many wonderful books that describe the MBTI and the principles behind it in detail. My favorites are the following.

Isabel Briggs Myers, *Gifts Differing*

An overview of type theory by one of the MBTI's creators.

David Keirsey, *Please Understand Me II*

Keirsey focuses on four core "temperaments" that underlie the sixteen possible types. His great contribution is showing how the different aspects of type operate in combination—for example, the significant differences between "intuitive thinkers" and "intuitive feelers." Although the book is somewhat dense, many clients find it to be a breakthrough analysis of how their minds work. (*Please Understand Me II* is an expanded version of the original book, *Please Understand Me*, which is also still sold.)

Paul Tieger and Barbara Barron-Tieger, *Do What You Are*

Practical and easy to read, with specific suggestions about occupations most suitable to different types.

The Enneagram

Another archetype that can be used for career insight is the Enneagram, which is based on the assumption that there are nine core archetypes in human experience. Of books that deal with the Enneagram, I recommend:

Renee Baron and Elizabeth Wagele, *The Enneagram Made Easy*

Fun and light (lots of cartoons), but informative.

Don Richard Riso, *The Wisdom of the Enneagram*

Long and comprehensive, but illuminating.

Helen Palmer, *The Enneagram in Love and Work*

Along with Riso, one of the two major writers on the Enneagram. Somewhat more cheerful in outlook than Riso.

CHAPTER 8

How Relationships Matter

"Law is a people business," says Chris Palamountain, a partner in a commercial litigation firm. "Legal skills are people skills."

She explains further: "Being able to read other people and their needs in a situation is what allows you to figure out what they're going to be persuaded by and what is going to offend them. This is certainly a more crucial part of litigation practice than writing a brief."

In Chris's experience, the higher up she's gone, the more emotionally intelligent have been the attorneys she has met.

"When I started out litigating with the ACLU, we were litigating against local assistant U.S. attorneys in various districts. They were generally abrasive, aggressive, sort of swaggering, testosterone-laden, even when they were women. They seemed to be people who relied on having the power of the government behind them.

"But as we went to the circuit courts and then eventually to the Supreme Court, the quality of lawyering got much better, and a lot of this was because the lawyers themselves were better people. The opposing counsel had a lot more empathy and were much more reasonable in a lot of ways.

"I've also noticed this working in commercial litigation. The top law firm partners I work with are really fun to be around as people. They may be adversaries, but they are respected adversaries. They engage you. They express an interest in different people in the room. Even when they show their aggressive side, they're showing it in a way that is not offensive. They're able to display charisma in a way that you can't help but admire and like."

Chris's observation of the role of emotional intelligence in law is borne out by research in other fields. The more senior managers become, the more they are helped or hindered by their level of emotional intelligence. Images of successful CEOs as tough-talking, no-nonsense autocrats— think Donald Trump, Jack Welch, and Dick Cheney—are the archetypes of a dying species. Most successful professional people are pretty developed emotionally; if they're not, their success has come despite, not because of, their less appealing qualities.

Emotional intelligence, a term coined by pioneering psychologist Daniel Goleman, is a major field unto itself. It's spawned a rich literature, along with a lot of consultants. In Goleman's formulation, emotional intelligence has two domains: *personal competence*, which includes self-awareness and self-management; and *social competence*, which includes social awareness and relationship management.

Goleman and his colleagues have spent a great deal of effort attempting to quantify the value of emotional intelligence. One method they have used is examining the competency requirements set forth by more than five hundred organizations—global companies, health care organizations, academic institutions, government agencies, and even a religious order. These competency requirements are the institutions' own assessments of the characteristics required for success by executives and leaders. One significant discovery of this research was that emotional intelligence becomes increasingly important the higher individuals rise in their careers—far more important than technical skills.

Goleman explains that while it takes a relatively high IQ to earn advanced degrees in the first place, "There is little or no systematic selection pressure when it comes to emotional intelligence, and so there is a much wider range of variation among executives. That lets superiority in these capabilities count far more than IQ when it comes to star leadership performance."

You do need a baseline of intelligence to become a lawyer. But once you become a lawyer, your success vis-à-vis other lawyers is not going to be determined primarily by intelligence. As one senior partner says, "To be successful, you can't be too stupid, but the level of intelligence that's required is a level of intelligence that most people that have gone to law school would have."

One type of emotional intelligence that is especially relevant to success, and arguably happiness, is the ability to build meaningful relationships.

Exercise: Getting Curious about Your Colleagues

Answer the following questions about two of your colleagues. For the first person, select someone who is considered senior to you professionally, or otherwise in a powerful position. For the second person, think of someone who is considered junior or subordinate to you. If you don't know the answers, ask!

1. What does your colleague like most about his or her job?

2. What is he or she proud of?

3. What demotivates him or her?

4. What makes his or her day?

5. What misconceptions, if any, do others have about him or her?

6. How would he or she like to grow?

7. What is a skill he or she has that everyone can benefit from?

8. When is his or her birthday?

Relationships Get Work Done

Every professional person has relationships. If you have strong, rich, and extensive relationships, you will improve the quality of your work and life—and if you have weak, superficial, and restricted relationships, you will hobble yourself.

"A huge amount of corporate work is finding ways to get other people to work with you effectively, and most of the time you have no actual authority over them," says Frank Villalpando, a senior associate who works in the capital markets group of a white-shoe New York firm. "You're competing for resources because your deal is by no means the only thing going on in their lives. And whether people want to be your resources depends on whether they like you, whether they respect you, whether they feel respected by you, whether you take time to understand their other constraints, whether you actually do care about them as people rather than seeing them as some kind of functionary."

He explains how relationships affected his own evolution as an attorney.

"When I was starting out, I felt detached from my work. It seemed to require about 20 percent of who I really was. I was completely fungible—any reasonably intelligent person could be substituted in to do the same work."

However, there was a time when Frank didn't feel that way—when he was at the financial printers. "Most people hate going to the printers, since you end up spending about three full days and nights together hammering out all the details of the prospectus that no one has really paid attention to so far. You're in a room with clients, lawyers, accountants, bankers, and support people, most of whom have come kicking and screaming. But I was good at running the printers. I ran a tight ship, but I made things fun. I liked it.

"I remember sitting in this room at two in the morning with my clients, who were from Venezuela. We were making sure the Spanish version matched the English version. They were exhausted and becoming distracted. I kept saying things like, 'Focus! Focus!' and 'Five more pages and you can have a cigarette! Or ice cream! Or a Scotch!' And after a while, they were the ones shouting, 'Focus! Focus!' It sounds kind of lame, but it was actually a really fun bonding time.

"And that's how I got noticed, I suppose. Senior people recognized that I did solid legal work *and* was someone people liked working with. Not just clients and lawyers and bankers, but the support staff as well. Other lawyers came to me for advice on how to deal with the word-processing department. They would get into these strange passive-aggressive feuds that they didn't know how to get out of. Whereas I always took time to get to know the secretarial and other support staff, and liked them as people, and never had any of those problems.

"As a result, I got more interesting work, and more responsibility. Somewhat to my surprise, I started liking my work a lot and feeling good about it."

The Role of Others in Your Success

As Keith Ferrazzi points out in his book *Never Eat Alone*, self-sufficiency is largely a myth. Other people play active roles in our own success.

Consider an accomplishment that you're really proud of. Now think about the ways others made that success possible.

For example, one of Gabriel's greatest accomplishments is that he learned to speak Spanish fluently. It's a way for him to connect with other people around the world. He worked hard for years and years to attain his current level of fluency. He's proud of what he's achieved. But he doesn't find it difficult to describe how others contributed to his success in various ways:

- My mom, who always talked about how fun it would be to learn a foreign language
- My Uncle Mike, who didn't laugh when I told him, at age ten, that I was "a citizen of the world"
- My high school Spanish teacher, Mr. Valadez, who drilled us in the Spanish-language rules of spelling and accent
- My grandmother, who spent most of her life in a farming town in the South but sent me $500 for my high school graduation and told me to see the world
- My host-family brother and sister when I studied in Cuernavaca, who carefully listened as I tried to explain myself in a foreign language and never showed signs of impatience or boredom

Exercise: How You're Connected

Think for a moment of a few of the accomplishments you are proud of, personally or professionally. List five of them.

1. _____
2. _____
3. _____
4. _____
5. _____

Circle one of these accomplishments that stands out for you. Now, ask yourself: What role did other people play in enabling you to achieve it? List five ways that others helped you in this accomplishment.

1. _____
_____
2. _____
_____

3. _____

   _____

4. _____

   _____

5. _____

   _____

Ingredients of Solid Relationships

All relationships are based on mutuality of interest. You have certain needs, and the other person has certain other needs. A good working relationship results when both parties get their needs met—end of story. Every relationship is in some ways a negotiation of how this is going to happen.

Relationships stay undeveloped or dysfunctional partly when we don't think deeply enough about other people's needs, or even our own. Once we think more deeply about them, we have room for growth.

The way this actually works is twofold:

1. In order to understand someone else's needs, you have to be curious. You have to wonder, ask, and listen.
2. In order to create an actual relationship, you also need to share. This is sometimes referred to as "transparency." You have to be willing to express your own needs, interests, and vulnerabilities.

It's the two practices working together that create connection. If someone is highly curious about you but shares nothing about himself, it can feel a little weird, as if you're being interviewed. (Lawyers, accustomed to asking questions, sometimes fall into this habit.) Conversely, if someone shares a lot about herself but is not curious about you, it's no fun either—you're just the audience.

Exercise: Identifying Needs

Return to the two people you wrote about in the "Getting Curious" exercise above. Now answer the following questions, which refer to needs— both theirs and yours. Note that mutuality of interest applies regardless of power levels. Again, if you don't know the answers—ask!

1. What are his or her main *professional* needs?

2. What are his or her main *personal* needs?

3. How can you help this person meet these needs?

4. What are *your* main professional needs?

5. What are your main personal needs?

6. How can this person help you meet your needs?

7. Given your answers to the above, what changes might you make in your interactions?

Box 8-1. Example: Identifying Needs

Carol, a sole practitioner, considered her needs and those of her office manager, Jill.

1. *Jill's main professional needs*
   - Decent salary
   - Appreciation
   - Being respected as a professional person, including opportunities to learn more
   - Proper resources to get her job done

2. *Jill's main personal needs*
   - Ability to leave at 4 p.m. to pick up her daughter
   - Occasional flexibility for medical and school appointments

3. *How I can help Jill meet her needs*
   - Provide the office equipment and software she needs to do a really good job, instead of getting by with outdated things
   - Write a clear list of tasks at the beginning of each week or day so she can plan her own schedule effectively (rather than throwing things at her throughout the day)
   - Hire a part-time assistant for her

4. *My main professional needs*
   - Having my appointments efficiently booked
   - Having an intermediary between me and the world
   - Having all administrative tasks handled so I can focus on revenue-generating work

5. *My main personal needs*
- Periods of quiet time (both to focus on my work and because I'm an introvert)

6. *How Jill can help me meet my needs*
- Keep doing what she's doing
- Aggregate her questions and requests so that she can ask me all at once rather than dropping in five times an hour

7. *Given my answers to the above, what changes might I make in our interactions?*
- I realize that Jill's continuing professional development helps both of us, so I want to be more supportive of that.

Relationships and Thinking Like a CEO

How any institution stays alive and thrives is determined by its business model. For a commercial enterprise, the business model is how it makes a profit. For a nonprofit or governmental organization, it is how the entity maintains necessary funding. No matter how competent and hard-working you are, if you do not have a clear understanding of the business model of your organization, at some point what you are doing may drift away from what the organization actually needs. You may then run into problems.

The connection that the business model has with your professional relationships is that it determines, in part, *what others need from you.* These other individuals and entities are, in the language of our age, your *stakeholders.*

A key question that any professional should always keep in mind is, "What are my stakeholders' needs?" You should not wait until your stakeholders come to you to explain their needs—it may not occur to them ever to do so. Instead, you need to make a practice of anticipating their needs or, better yet, asking about them.

A shorthand way of approaching this is the idea of "thinking like a CEO." This means inhabiting the mindset of the person whose job it is to think of the survival and progress of the organization as a whole:

- If you work for a law firm, thinking like a CEO means asking yourself what your bosses are trying to accomplish related to the underlying need of the firm to make money.
- If you work for a nonprofit or governmental organization, thinking like a CEO means putting yourself in the position of the

executive director, asking how the people or entities that provide funding are assessing the value of the organization.

- If you are a sole practitioner, thinking like a CEO means asking what is important to your clients or potential clients.
- If you are working as an in-house lawyer for a company, thinking like a CEO means asking how the work you do relates to the current business objectives of the company.

Ultimately, thinking like a CEO comes down to the question: What are the actual needs of the people for whom I work, and how can I help to satisfy them?

For example, a partner explains how this works in the context of a large firm: "One of the misunderstandings associates have about partners is the idea that once you make partner you have it made. Actually, that's when the real rat race begins. The first six to ten years after becoming partner determine whether you're going to make it or not. Either you're going to get fired— or be stuck in the backwaters forever, tolerated if you do the work of some senior partner—or you're going to break out.

"To break out, you need your own client following. You get clients either because you're their main business contact or because you're a great expert in a particular area, like M&A, capital markets, or litigation. Whatever category partners are in, they need loyal associates who are really going to do the work and make sure the clients are happy and make sure that those partners shine."

According to this attorney, regardless of their own levels of emotional intelligence, partners are quite attuned to the ways that associates build relationships. She explains: "The worst mistake a midlevel or senior associate can make is to try to shine by putting down the partner he or she is working for. There's no way you can survive if you do that. Another mistake they can make is thinking that they're so smart and cool, they can just do it all on their own. A different kind of mistake is to flip from mentor to mentor. You might do it once or twice, but eventually you're going to get a reputation as a disloyal creep."

So how does thinking like a CEO affect the kind of relationships you build?

"When you think like a CEO or like a senior partner, you're going to understand that you have to run a business, you have to have a team, and therefore you can't be this Lone Ranger type. You have to fit into a larger business goal and make yourself useful in that context as a loyal team member."

Relationships Enrich Your Life and Make You Happy

Strong relationships work in another important way—they often determine whether you are happy or not.

"It was my relationships with other associates that inspired me to stick through the tough, early years," says Jocelyn Gutierrez, a transactional lawyer. Jocelyn works of counsel to a 100-lawyer firm based in Los Angeles. She telecommutes between her home outside Las Vegas and the firm's headquarters in Los Angeles. Her part-time arrangement allows her to have a balanced life even as she continues in her role as the primary breadwinner for her family of five.

Jocelyn didn't start off with a vision of how to do this. Her law school classmates and early colleagues marked her as a short-timer. She didn't disagree. "I couldn't see how I was going to keep this up. I didn't like the work at first, and I was unwilling to put in the hours other people were cranking out. It was so difficult the first several years that it helped just being with other people who were going through it."

Relationships not only sustained her, but were also the source of useful ideas.

"For the particular arrangement I have now, I was inspired by a friend who created a part-time partnership arrangement at her firm. I hadn't thought it was possible to have kids and continue to practice. And on a different level, I've been inspired to have balance because I had friends who insisted on getting it. My friend, Arina, has always worked incessantly, but she has also always managed to carve out time for flamenco and salsa classes. When you actually see people do things like that, you realize that they are possible.

"In my case, I don't think it was until years five and six of practice that I finally got a sense of what I knew, and started getting rewarded for that. I also think what's been so critical for me in maintaining my career is the fact that it was never just about the job—a good percentage of my life, my self-worth, and my interests have come out of my relationships and my kids.

"It's interesting that things have worked out the way they did. The people I knew who were most intense at first seem to have flamed out, whereas I'm in a good place professionally. My clients like me, I feel confident about my abilities, and I'm able to make good money."

Laila Sharif, who left a partnership at a national firm to start her own criminal defense shop, echoes the importance of relationships with people who *get* you. "My most important relationships are the ones I developed in college and law school," she says. "I'm the kind of person who actually enjoys reading my alumni magazine. These friends are the most important examples for me of thoughtful, interesting people. I think that because they knew me before I ever became a lawyer, they keep me in touch with my core values as a person. I never feel boxed in when I'm around them, and it gives me a kind of freedom to keep developing."

Whom you hang out with determines in part what you consider normal and what you think is possible. This is a relevant point when thinking about ways to achieve balance. If you hang out with people who work impossible hours and build lives around the idea that balance is unattainable, it probably won't seem all that possible.

Adam Zucker, a partner in a small general practice outside of Philadelphia, observes: "There are some people for whom work is their life. Their lives are doing deals, closing deals, trying cases, and that's their identity. They're not as comfortable functioning outside the office as they are inside the office. At the same time, there are other types of people as well—the ones they call 'omega kids' in school, the ones who are inwardly directed. Those are the ones who will say, 'It's okay to take Thursday off to take my daughter to the aquarium.'

"When I first started out, I was with a large firm and worked very long hours. I was part of that crowd that thought it was macho to work until 11 or 12 at night. I'm not part of that crowd anymore."

Exercise: Sketch Your Circle of Support

On a blank page, draw a circle filling about half the space. Make a mark in the middle of the circle denoting yourself.

The interior of the circle is the space for people who positively support you at this stage in your life. They like you, approve of you, give good advice, and support your truest self. The closer their names are to the center, the more you can rely on them.

The exterior of the circle is for people who don't support you at this stage in your life. This can include naysayers, people who express "loving" doubts, emotionally limited people, and general troublemakers.

The perimeter of the circle is for people who could go either way (a lot of family members end up on the line).

Jot down names of people in your life according to where they fall in your circle of support.

Several exercises in this book are intended to make you aware of how people in your world can be resources for you. This exercise is partly intended to alert you to the ways that some people in your life may hold you back.

The Value of Non-lawyers

Lawyers whose networks consist solely or primarily of other lawyers are marginalized without knowing it. They are stuck in a professional and personal ghetto, cut off from other perspectives, energies, and connections. Excess specialization can keep you in a box.

I see this most commonly in lawyers who are thinking of changing careers. What's the biggest barrier? The fact that most of their relationships are with other lawyers. They lack information on how to market themselves in other industries, or even what the requirements are. Because they are not hanging out with people who have actually made a transition, they often have a negative assessment about the prospects of making one. Monocultures are rarely creative.

Poorly developed networks are one reason why law as a field is slow to change. Since everyone else is doing and saying the same things, the status quo is easy to justify. Problems, such as incredibly high attorney turnover at major firms, are seen as "normal" or "inevitable" partly because lawyers in decision-making positions do not interact enough with people in other sectors who are handling similar problems much more effectively.

Some of your best ideas, energies, and connections will come from non-lawyers.

Exercise: Diversify Your Crowd

If you are spending most of your time with lawyers, you are limiting your intake of fresh ideas, perspectives, and energies. The problem is homogeneity, which is not anything specific to lawyers. Actors who hang out just with actors have the same problem, for example.

Write the names of ten people you like who are *not* lawyers.

1. _____

2. _____

3. _____

4. _____

5. _____

6. _____

7. _____

8. _____

9. _____

10. _____

Pick five of these non-lawyers to hang out with over the next month.

Good Relationships Mitigate Not-So-Good Relationships

Strengthening certain relationships can help you to mitigate the negative effects of others.

For example, Frank Villalpando discovered that the stronger his client relationships became, the less intrusive his relationships with partners were. "As I developed my knowledge and formed longer-term bonds with clients, they started coming to me directly rather than calling the partners. Even though I sometimes felt insecure about my knowledge level, I gradually realized that the partners often didn't know that much, either. At first I would include them on calls and meetings, but I came to see that, really, the clients just wanted me."

Frank gradually gained more control over his schedule. "Over time, my life improved because I basically cut out the middleman. There were no higher-ups telling me to do rush jobs over the weekend that they wouldn't even look at for several days. I could directly assess what the client needed, and get it done in a rational way. And actually the partners liked not being as involved, since they could be free to worry about other things."

ADDITIONAL EXERCISES

Attending to relationships is a core principle of professional life, not an occasional activity. That said, engaging in some relationship-enhancing activities is a great way to make this principle a fundamental part of your life! Here are five quick and fun relationship-building activities.

Make unsolicited introductions. List three pairs of people you will introduce to each other:

1. Introduce _____ and _____
2. Introduce _____ and _____
3. Introduce _____ and _____

Buy birthday cards. Make a list of five people to send birthday cards to. At least three should be people with whom you have a working relationship. Look up their birthdays. Go out and buy five cards at once. Put them somewhere easily located and mark your calendar to remind you when to send them. You can fill them all out ahead of time, or wait until the right week rolls around.

1. Birthday greeting _____
2. Birthday greeting _____
3. Birthday greeting _____
4. Birthday greeting _____
5. Birthday greeting _____

Note: this is the only exercise in this book that is highly gendered—a lot of women reading this book already do things like this and very few of the men do.

Write after-the-fact thank-you notes. Take out your nice paper or card sets and write three short notes to people who have helped you in the past. Let them know you've been thinking about them, and say something about how their help has been beneficial. It could be teachers, friends, relatives, or colleagues—and don't forget Mom! Mail them.

1. Thank you to _____
2. Thank you to _____
3. Thank you to _____

Create a cool-things-to-share folder. Take a plain folder and label it "Cool Things." Start filling it with articles, announcements of events, film reviews, and other items you think friends or acquaintances might be interested in. Share the items. (You can also do this electronically through email and hyperlinks.)

Host a salon. Plan a party or dinner. However, instead of inviting your usual guests for the usual scene, invite a specific group of people who have an interest in a theme that is compelling to you. Any subject is possible: travel, a particular kind of career exploration, a political interest. For extra fun, ask one or two people to do a show-and-tell about a particular area of expertise they have. If your guests work in the same world, post little reminders that shoptalk is *verboten!*

READING LIST

Daniel Goleman, *Primal Leadership*

Since publishing his now-classic work *Emotional Intelligence* a number of years ago, Goleman and his colleagues have continued their research into the applications of EI to leadership. This popular book describes five distinct leadership styles consistent with high levels of emotional intelligence.

CHAPTER 9

The Networking Chapter

You can't have a book about careers without a chapter on networking. There's a rule about that. First, though, a story.

Several years ago, Marci Alboher, a lawyer who had been practicing for about ten years, decided to try to become a professional writer. The first inklings of this goal emerged when she was living in Hong Kong, working as in-house counsel for *Reader's Digest*.

Marci's life in Hong Kong was interesting and fun. Because she worked only three days per week, she was able to take advantage of Hong Kong's geographic location to travel throughout the Southeast Asian region. She started sending emails about her experiences to an extended list. Many people shared her reports with their other friends, and a few of these folks were journalists and writers. More than one complimented her on her talents for writing and observation. "You could be a writer," she was told.

When she returned to the United States, Marci took a class in freelance journalism at the New School in New York City. During that course, she sold a freelance piece to the *New York Times*. It felt great. Marci was hooked.

However, she was aware that one submission, or even a handful of them, did not constitute a career. She was still working as a lawyer, in a new job that she didn't particularly like. Marci realized that if she was really going to become a writer, she needed to start living like one, and one way to live like one was to start hanging out more with writers. Marci had known a lot of lawyers, financiers, and consultants. She had run across diplomats and entrepreneurs. But she didn't know many writers or journalists. She needed to change this.

On the final session of her class at the New School, she and two other classmates found themselves agreeing on the need to keep up the momentum. They made a pact to create a transition-to-writing group. They would set goals, hold each other accountable, and support each other in acquiring these new identities. It was a writing group, but even more than that, it was a goal-achieving group.

For more than a year, the group met every week. Outside of the group, they had other lives and identities. But inside it, they related to each other as people wanting to become writers and, increasingly, as authors.

Several years down the road, all three women are established as writers. If you met them, it wouldn't occur to you that they'd ever been anything else. Marci herself recently published a book on careers and writes an online column for the *New York Times*.

Marci is an extremely energetic, capable person. Meeting her, you can see why she would be successful in this career, or any career. But the link between the life she had and the life she wanted was other people. She wasn't in the right network to pursue her ambitions, so she created it.

Awkward? Perhaps—Essential? Yes

Networking is not everyone's favorite word.

In her wonderful book on creativity, *The Creative Habit: Learn It and Use It for Life*, choreographer Twyla Tharp uses her gym workout as an interesting metaphor for the process of engagement.

Ms. Tharp, now in her sixties, wakes up each day at 5:00 a.m. in order to work out with her trainer at 6. She makes clear that she never actually *wants* to work out each gray morning. But she overrides her desires, every single day.

The hard part is not the workout. It's the decision to *do* the workout. "The workout begins," Tharp writes, "when I get into the taxi."

So it is with networking. Networking begins when you say hi, pick up the phone, or click "send." For most people, the hardest part is this first step. Once you actually initiate the human connection, it gets easier. Not for everyone, but for most. It's picking up the phone and dialing that's hard.

There are a number of books and networking experts who will tell you that networking is not difficult if you know certain secrets. They are wrong. Networking requires making efforts beyond what we would do unselfconsciously. Like watching your diet or starting an exercise program, networking is good for you, even though it might not feel so fun the first day you try it.

Because networking is all about accessing your weak ties (more on that later), it's always about stretching out of your comfort zone. This can be tough. Says one career advisor at a major law school who is a lawyer herself, "When you mention networking to students, more than half of them visibly cringe."

What's the benefit of networking? You access ideas, energies, perspectives, connections, and possibilities that don't exist within the bounds of your known life. You get a chance to learn about others and help them, and they get a chance to learn about and help you. You live more.

"Everything I do is about building relationships," says Toni Fine, an assistant dean at Fordham Law School who runs the school's international law programs. "In my work, it's important to develop close relationships not only with the people with whom I work but also with whoever walks into my office, whether it's a judge from Korea or a lawyer from Brazil. Networking is really important for me and for my students and for the program development. It's something I have to do 24/7. And it's something we encourage our students to do. We talk about networking from the minute they arrive—which is a challenge because some of them find it unseemly and awkward. But there's no way around it. To find the opportunities that make use of their skills and energies, they have to be out in the world connecting with people."

To live as a creative lawyer, you have to network.

Building, Maintaining, and Accessing Relationships

Networking involves three different things:

1. *Building* relationships
2. *Maintaining* relationships
3. *Accessing* relationships

In the early part of your career, and when you switch careers, specialty areas, or interests, you need to focus on building relationships. The perspective here is long-term. You are making deposits into a savings account that will build over time.

As you advance in your career, you need to focus on maintaining relationships. You will naturally accumulate a large number of contacts; the task is to find ways to keep the important ones alive and meaningful.

Throughout your career, you need to access relationships. Accessing relationships involves asking for things—information, opinions, feedback, recommendations, introductions, fix-ups, time, money, opportunities, and so on—requests that reflect all the ways that people interact professionally and personally. Probably most people find it difficult to ask for things. Even people who are accustomed to asking for things within the confines of their roles—senior managers, for example—are usually uncomfortable asking for things outside of these roles.

I once had breakfast with a very senior and extremely well-connected lawyer in New York. A man about his age came up to our table to greet him. They exchanged greetings and the man turned to go back to his companion. After taking a step or two, he stopped and, somewhat sheepishly, turned to the lawyer I was meeting with.

"You know," the man began, "I was wondering. . . . My daughter is in her third year of law school and—if it wouldn't be an imposition—she would love to talk to you about the law some time." His face reddened.

"No problem," my dining companion said. "Just have her give me a call."

Gleeful, the man returned to his table.

That's Dr. So-and-so, the lawyer explained, adding that he was the head of one of New York's leading teaching hospitals.

Asking for things doesn't always feel easy. But you can do it!

Building Relationships on Purpose *Is Okay*

With my colleagues at Next Step Partners, I've conducted scores of workshops on networking. Frequently the audiences are MBA students, who you might think would easily embrace this business-y concept, but in fact they frequently resist it.

One exercise we do relates to networking perspectives. Students are grouped around the room according to the networking perspective they most identify with: "Networking is fun," "Networking is manipulative," and so forth.

Every time I've done this workshop, someone in the pro-networking camp will say something like, "I just like meeting people and learning about them, so I like networking."

In response, someone from the anti-networking camp will say, "I like meeting people, too, and if I meet people naturally, that's fine. But networking is all about having fake conversations and meeting people for the sole purpose of trying to get something from them."

I draw two points from these interactions. The first is that everyone has relationships and almost everyone finds some satisfaction in the process of building relationships. The second is that many people believe that relationships should just happen, and if you make proactive efforts to build them, they are inauthentic.

This is just wrong. The distinction between personal and professional networking is a false one. There's nothing the matter with trying to meet people on purpose. Actually, we do this all the time. If we're single, we ask people for help meeting potential partners, and if we're in a relationship, we ask people for advice on how to deal with those relationships. Most of our friendships and other social relationships come as a result of networking—some kind of introduction through an existing relationship.

The Strength of Weak Ties

If you made a list of all the people you know in life, they could be put into two categories: strong ties and weak ties.

Strong ties are people with whom you have recurring exchange. You see them reasonably often. You know what's going on with them. You exchange information on a regular basis.

Weak ties are everyone else. One group is people you know, but with whom you have infrequent contact. Think of your law school classmates, college roommates, former neighbors, clients from previous years, rarely seen relatives. Another group is people you don't know that well. These include new acquaintances, people you met at conferences, a new neighbor, a lecturer you met once, an adversary with whom you've had one or two interactions.

A large amount of academic research has been done over several decades on how social networks function. One of the best-known studies was conducted in the mid-1970s by a sociologist named Mark Granovetter. His subject was how people actually got jobs. Granovetter found that people who relied on their weak ties ended up getting more job offers, with higher salaries, than people who relied on their strong ties. These weak ties were typically distant acquaintances, not close friends and not family members.

How is it that weak ties are, in the end, more helpful to you than strong ties? The most important reason is that your strong ties often have the same ties and information you do. Weak ties live in different worlds and therefore have access to whole different worlds of people and information. Weak ties collectively present a lot more diversity, which gives you more possibilities.

There are other reasons that complement this one. In my experience, weak ties are somewhat less stressful to contact than strong ties. Without a strong preexisting relationship, there is less to screw up. People are often freer about their desires and ambitions when they talk to relative strangers. Another reason is that your strong ties may have a vested idea of who you are and what you're all about. As Herminia Ibarra writes in her wonderful book on career transition, *Working Identity*, "Our close contacts don't just blind us, they bind us to outdated identities." Strong ties may be unable to picture you accomplishing those changes, or they may feel personally threatened by the prospect of your changing.

The idea that you need to access your weak ties can be a little bit scary to people, but also liberating. "When people would talk about networking," a client in Seattle once told me, "I always thought, 'I can never do this, because I don't have that many close friends.' But I have a *very* long list of people that I kind of know!"

Exercise: List Your Strong and Weak Ties

In the diagram below start writing down the names of the people in your network. Put yourself in the center of your diagram. Write the names of your strong ties in the inner circle, your weak ties in the middle circle, and your weaker ties in the outermost circle. Go big—consider:

- Colleagues
- Clients
- Friends
- Relatives
- Contacts of your spouse, partner, or children
- Former classmates
- Former teachers and professors

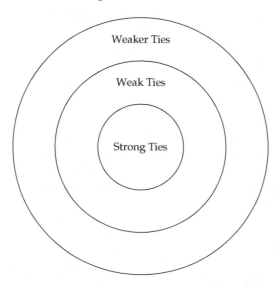

Figure 9-1. Chart of Strong and Weak Ties

- Neighbors
- Professional affiliations
- Religious affiliations
- Gym acquaintances
- Hobby/vocation colleagues
- Random contacts (e.g., airplane seatmates, fellow tour group participants)
- Famous or semifamous people you've come across

Assessing Your Network

So, how *is* your network?

Let's answer with another question: Whom do you want to be hanging out with? Given your professional and personal goals, what sort of people should you know?

You might be on the right path, or you may be way off.

Exercise: Analyze Your Network

Take a look at your filled-out networking radar screen. Then write out answers to the following questions.

1. What are my short-term career goals (1–3 years)? _____
   _____
   _____

2. What are my longer-term career goals (3–10 years)? _____
   _____
   _____

3. Given my career goals, what kind of people should be in my network? _____
   _____
   _____

4. Given my goals, what are the strengths of my network? _____
   _____
   _____

5. Given my goals, how do I need to develop my network further? __
   _____
   _____

6. What are five specific actions I can take toward this development?

- _____
- _____
- _____
- _____
- _____

Box 9-1. Example: Analyze Your Network

Nicole, who works in legal marketing and ultimately wants to run her own talent management agency, answered these questions as follows.

1. *What are my short-term career goals (1–3 years)?*
   I expect to continue doing law firm marketing. I'd like to improve my knowledge of marketing techniques, get management experience, and generally expand my business skills.

2. *What are my longer-term career goals (3–10 years)?*
   To move into talent management and eventually have my own agency.

3. *Given my career goals, what kind of people should be in my network?*
   Creative types, including artists, musicians, actors, and other entertainers, and people who work on the business side of entertainment, like agents, producers, and financiers.

4. *Given my goals, what are the strengths of my network?*
   I know a lot of artists of different kinds, and a few lawyers who do entertainment law. I have an unusual talent for meeting celebrities.

5. *Given my goals, how do I need to develop my network further?*
   I need to meet people who are actually doing the kind of work I want to do. Within my arts circles, I need to focus on people who are undiscovered enough that they would want to work with me, and talented enough that they could be really big!

6. *What are five specific actions I can take toward this development?*
   - Go to an entertainment law conference
   - Go to the Sundance Film Festival

- Go to the Cannes Film Festival (why not?!)
- Take a class at UCLA related to this interest
- Start introducing myself to new artistic people as a lawyer interested in representing people

MP   **Master Plan Intervention!**

Fill out the "Network Assessment" section of the Master Plan template in the appendix.

READING LIST

Keith Ferrazzi, *Never Eat Alone*

The new classic on networking. Not everyone will relate to the highly energetic Mr. Ferrazzi. However, he convincingly shows how all networking is fundamentally relationship building, and how relationships are the core to how we live. The book is filled with interesting stories and lots of tips. Depending on your personality, you will probably find anywhere from 20 to 80 percent of the book useful. Even at the lower end, it's well worth reading.

Malcolm Gladwell, *The Tipping Point*

Gladwell's colossal best-seller is a study about how certain types of people manage to have highly influential roles in society. A key part of this analysis is his description of three influential types of individuals—"connectors," "mavens," and "persuaders." He includes a very clear explanation of phenomena such as the "strength of weak ties" and other networking concepts.

Herminia Ibarra, *Working Identity*

Another reason to read Ibarra's book (also discussed in the reading list for chapter 11) is that she shows how meaningful career transition strongly depends on the extent to which individuals manage to meet people outside of their normal professional circles. Lots of good examples.

CHAPTER 10

Mindful Communications

When I was in the Foreign Service, one of my entering classmates was a dynamic woman named Barb Zigli, a journalist originally from Ohio. Barb was smart, peppy, friendly, down-to-earth, clear-headed, and action oriented—all the characteristics you might think of when hearing a name like Barb Zigli. Our entering class spent a great deal of time during our training sampling various Washington, D.C., restaurants—Ethiopian one night, Afghan another, Malaysian another. Barb regularly took over the function of organizing dinner outings, as well as museum trips and outdoor expeditions. Whenever one of us had a vague tingle to do something fun, we'd float the idea by Barb to get her to kick things into high gear.

I once commented to Barb how great it was that someone so naturally peppy and group oriented was part of our class.

"Oh, no," she said. "Actually I'm not like this at all. Before I joined the Foreign Service, I never did things like this. I just went along if other people organized things. But I never volunteered.

"But after our class started up, I wondered, 'What would happen if I just acted as if it was my nature to do this sort of thing?' and that's what I did. And I guess it worked."

Why does this story start off a chapter called "Mindful Communications"? Because words partly determined how Barb affected the world around her, and when she changed the types of things she said, she changed her actions and then her life. She put forth what she wanted, and the world responded. Barb is now the cultural affairs officer for the

U.S. Embassy in Beijing, the latest in a string of postings in China and Russia.

This principle works for organizing group dinners to area restaurants, and it works for managing your career throughout your life. The way you communicate *matters*. And when you are mindful about what your message is, and how you convey it, the rewards are far greater.

How Communications Make or Break You

As a youngster, I found the word *communications* to be very vague. I didn't know what it meant exactly. I suspected it didn't mean much. While adults frequently advised that good communications were important and that breakdowns in communication were problematic, these statements seemed obvious and unimportant. I regarded communications as something pretty basic, sort of like tying your shoes. Once you mastered some basic techniques, you pretty much had it down. You couldn't go much higher. I didn't understand how communications could be a whole major in college.

A couple of decades into adulthood, *I get it*. Probably 70 to 80 percent of my work as a coach deals with communication in various forms. I see how communications, effective or otherwise, determine our lives and relationships. Words, tone, timing, energy, physical expressiveness—these core elements create the atmosphere in which we all live. There are endless chemistries and variations. What you say and how you say it mean everything. I'm a total convert.

Good communications enable people to connect and understand one another. What this comes down to is people knowing how to communicate who they are and where they are going in their lives. This simple formulation can lead to a million complex permutations, but those are the basic elements.

However, communicating this information in a manner that works is not the easiest thing in the world. Generally speaking, good communications requires mindfulness. You have to think about what you are going to say and, occasionally, practice it.

What Do You Talk about When You Talk about Yourself?

Most professional people talk easily about their firms, colleagues, clients, services, or products. Talking about themselves is another matter. What do you talk about when you talk about yourself?

Exercise: What Do You Say?

Answer the following questions, either out loud or in writing.

1. *Situation:* A stringer for the *New York Times* is interviewing you. She asks, "What do you do?"

   Your answer: _____

   _____

   _____

   _____

   _____

2. *Situation:* You're on a flight to London and have been unexpectedly upgraded to first class. Your seatmate is Richard Branson, founder of Virgin Atlantic. After offering you some of his heated nuts, he sits back and says, "So, tell me about yourself."

   Your answer: _____

   _____

   _____

   _____

   _____

3. *Situation:* You are meeting with a person who has the ability to influence your career development—either a senior person in your existing organization, a hiring manager at another firm, or a potential client. She asks, "What's next for you?"

   Your answer: _____

   _____

   _____

   _____

   _____

4. *Situation:* At a lavish charitable function, you are seated next to a key mover and shaker, someone known for his incredible ability to connect cool, influential people. After learning a bit about your personal interests, he says, "How interesting! What can I do to help?"

   Your answer: _____

   _____

   _____

   _____

   _____

What You Say When You Talk about Yourself

So, how were your answers? Were they memorable? Did you feel that an interesting conversation was about to kick off?

Were you comfortable answering?

No one wants to be judged on the basis of a few words. But we *are* judged. And we judge other people. We go through life making quick assessments of what is worth our time, what is worthy of further investigation, who we like, who we don't. Hence, we need to have some good answers to some of the most common soft volleys of professional life:

- What do you do?
- Tell me about yourself.
- What are you looking for?
- What brought you here?
- What can I do for you?

"What do you do?" isn't a bad question. It means "Please start the conversation" and possibly "I'd like to learn more about you." (Sometimes it means "I'm standing next to you and feel I should ask you a question," but that is less common.)

These sorts of questions can be used to put you on the spot, to make you justify yourself, but usually that's not what's going on. Most often, the other person just wants to learn something about you. You're saying *something* in reply—what is it that you're saying?

The Positioning Statement

Good communication begins with self-awareness about who you are and what you want in life. The main work in communications preparation isn't anticipating what others will think of you—it's taking time to figure out what *you* think of you.

Your core communications tool is the positioning statement. Your positioning statement gets across your key messages about you. No matter what the situation, you do this by basically covering two themes:

1. Who you are
2. What you want

The first part helps the listener understand you and gives you credibility; the second lets the listener know how to help you. Note that "what you want" doesn't necessarily mean what you would like from the other person. It refers more to what you want from life, where you are going, and the ways you would like to develop.

The content that fills the positioning statement depends on who you are, where you are in life, and the context you in are.

Let's see a few examples.

Professional Development

First, let's consider what you talk about when you are talking about your professional development—where you are going as a professional, what you aspire to, what you've accomplished, how you seek to grow. Here are two illustrations.

New law graduate starting out at a big firm:

"Right now I have two major career goals: building my skills as a solid transactions lawyer and making some contribution to the broader community. I could use advice on how to be most effective in my role as a junior associate. And I would love to be introduced to people who are connected to organizations that work for immigrants rights or low-income communities."

Senior partner at management seminar:

"I'm a partner in a large Chicago firm and recently was named managing partner. While I'm very confident practicing law, I'm somewhat new to management. I'm attending this course because I'm interested in learning how other professional services firms have improved their internal management."

Career Transition

The next set of positioning statements are the type that are used in career transition—meeting new contacts, updating friends, or kicking off interviews. Note that the speakers are not giving their entire personal resume—they are focusing on what they want to be known for. It's crucial that they indicate the types of positions they seek—otherwise the other person has no idea how to help them.

Government lawyer wanting to go in-house:

"I have nine years' experience practicing law, since graduating from Northwestern Law School. I've worked both for government agencies and for private firms. I would love to apply my IP and negotiations skills in an in-house role with a multinational corporation. I'm especially interested in the pharmaceutical sector—companies like Pfizer or J&J—and the sports sector—for example, Reebok."

115

Back-to-work parent making career switch:

> "Before taking time off to raise my kids, I spent ten years as an M&A lawyer, advising banks and companies on major financial decisions. During the past few years, I've grown really impassioned about conservation and the threat of global warming. I'd love to use my fundraising skills and professional network to help an organization that focuses on issues like these, like Greenpeace, the Sierra Club, or a smaller entity."

Business Development

Business development conversations also require a solid positioning statement. Good communications are what distinguish random networking from meaningful interactions. There's a certain art here in being direct without being too pushy. A good strategy is to put forward what's of interest to you without specifying that the other person needs to be the one to satisfy those interests.

Solo practitioner soliciting business:

> "I'm a lawyer with my own shingle. I work with individuals, families, and small businesses. Basically, my job is to solve problems, whether that means negotiating employee contracts, purchasing real estate, dealing with ex-spouses, or fending off creditors. My clients are my friends and, on that note, I'm currently looking for more friends!"

Attorney checking in with a new contact at a major client:

> "I'm glad that things settled so painlessly—the best all-nighters are the ones you never have to do. It was great to get to know you in the past few months. Why don't we have lunch some time? I would love to hear about the kinds of things you're facing in your new position."

Personal Goals

Finally, one of the best occasions to use a positioning statement is in the furtherance of personal goals.

Bankruptcy lawyer seeking balance:

> "I'm a partner in small firm specializing in bankruptcy, on the creditor side. While I'm happy with how my career has progressed, I want to achieve better work/life balance. I have two small children

and want to be part of their growing up! I'd like to connect with other professionals who are juggling work and personal responsibilities and get some of their ideas."

Lawyer with dreams of television glory:

"I'm a writer and have developed several sample episodes for an adult cartoon series featuring trash-talking animals—it's basically *South Park* meets *Animal Planet*. My day job is working as a lawyer—I'm with one of the major firms downtown. Right now, I'm looking for additional collaborators to work on our cartoon project and am also shopping it out to different studios."

Exercise: Draft Your Positioning Statement

Using the area that most resonates with you, draft your positioning statement. You might have more than one, depending on your interests.

Positioning Statement Version #1:

_____

_____

_____

_____

_____

_____

_____

_____

Positioning Statement Version #2:

_____

_____

_____

_____

_____

_____

_____

MP

Master Plan Intervention!

Copy the two versions of your positioning statement over to the template in the appendix.

Creating Positioning Statements—Tips

While it's hard to sum yourself up in a few sentences, positioning statements improve with practice. Through feedback—the reactions of others and your own—you learn what works.

Let go of your stuff. Your positioning statement is a quick overview of who you are, as it relates to the particular conversation. It is not an oral version of your resume. Leave out the twists and turns of fate that have brought you to this point. Focus on what's relevant. For instance, if you spend all day doing insurance defense but want to join the board of an organization that works to combat violence against women, it might be more useful to talk about your law school clinical work than your job.

Help your audience understand. Your positioning statement should be understandable by more than an elite cabal. Saying you're a "'40 Act lawyer" is comprehensible to some people, but not to others. Add details that give a flavor of what you do: "I'm an immigration lawyer. What I really love about my job is helping to reunite families and getting people through a very difficult and scary system."

Consider who you are really representing. Your positioning statement will have different forms depending on who you are representing—yourself, your organization, an association, or another entity.

Talking about What You Want

Describing clearly what you want helps other people help you. If you make it sufficiently clear what you want, you won't even need to ask the other person for help. For example:

- "We're currently expanding our business and I'm reaching out to potential clients."
- "I've enjoyed working with your company and would love to get a sense of your expansion plans."
- "I'm making a shift from government to private work and would love feedback on how my skills transfer."
- "I'm trying to get a sense of the current timetable for Labor Certifications at the DHS."

There are a lot of things you might want, either personally or professionally. The thing you want might be quite hard to help with ("I want to go to medical school") or it might be quite easy ("I'm looking for a website to buy a car"). Ways others might help you include:

- new business with an existing client
- new business with a new client
- feedback on your work
- feedback on your resume
- intelligence about where the industry is going
- career advice
- information about a sector
- introductions to new people
- information about professional development opportunities
- learning how the other person has developed her career or business
- recommendation for a good babysitter

Having clarity about your core messages frees you to participate in meaningful conversations. In contrast, if you are figuring out what you are saying as you go along, you are probably not fully present in the conversation.

READING LIST

Phyllis Mindell, *How to Say It for Women: Communicating with Confidence and Power Using the Language of Success*

This is the one of the best books I've read on effective communications. The title notwithstanding, it's a book that can benefit everyone. The author reviews the verbal and nonverbal elements that form workplace communications.

Peter Block, *Flawless Consulting*

A major element to being successful at consulting, it turns out, is knowing how to communicate with your client on scope of work, deadlines, and money. A useful book for any service professional.

The books recommended in chapter 7, on managing type, are also insightful regarding communications challenges and techniques.

CHAPTER 11

Growth and the Habit of Experimentation

Criminals and Jewels

Coming from a family of police officers, Bridget O'Callaghan wanted to become a prosecutor. Graduating from law school in a difficult employment market, she was unable to enter that field directly and ended up getting work in a small maritime litigation firm. From there, she moved into another civil litigation firm, then another, and then to a boutique criminal defense firm run by a well-known attorney, where she focused on white-collar litigation. Although she was working on the side of the defense rather than the prosecution, she had a good platform from which to build her skills and credibility.

However, as she gained experience, Bridget's interests started to change. The actual work of representing defendants challenged her initial perspective. She discovered aspects of prosecution that she didn't like and in particular had problems with mandatory sentencing guidelines. She found value in working on behalf of the accused.

It wasn't the case, though, that her former passion had simply switched sides. What had happened was that Bridget's former legal passion had faded without a new passion to replace it. She felt lost and somewhat panicked. She needed something else, some new direction toward which she could expend her considerable energies.

During this period, Bridget investigated a number of alternatives. She considered other firms, in-house jobs, and nonprofit organizations. She interviewed for a legal position with the ASPCA—another great passion of hers was animal welfare. But the role wasn't right. She didn't see any clear choices.

While all of this was happening, something else was going on in Bridget's life.

"I had a piece of jewelry that was poorly made, and it broke. So one day I went to a jewelry supply store to get the materials to fix it. I thought, 'I could do a better job than whoever made this.'"

Bridget took a jewelry design class and began creating her own pieces. She was pleased with them and received numerous compliments. She began hanging out at jewelry supply stores and selling her pieces to acquaintances.

On a vacation to the Caribbean, she walked into a tony shop run by an elderly ex-Parisian couple with her samples and asked if they would be interested in carrying her pieces. They said yes. She started going to trade shows, set up a website, and checked out different suppliers. The idea of becoming a successful designer and businesswoman, something she had never previously considered, started feeling very appealing.

One day Bridget donated a piece to an auction benefiting a children's music education group. It raised enough to send a child musician to Japan. Bridget felt *great* about her contribution. Maybe this could be a way to contribute to the causes she cared about, such as animal welfare.

At the same time her jewelry hobby was turning into a jewelry business, her work environment was becoming increasingly stressful. She started interviewing for other law jobs again. At the same time, she wondered if she should try something more dramatic—like leaving law and focusing entirely on the jewelry business.

Bridget didn't know how the different elements of her life should fit together, if they did at all. What did it mean that she'd invested so many years into a career and now was most excited by something that had nothing to do with it? Was she a businesswoman on the rise or just a lucky hobbyist? Should she try to reestablish her legal career, or bid it good riddance?

What Happens When Life Changes?

A good life is almost never static. The world decides to change, or something inside of us changes, without our prior approval. Growth happens.

Sometimes we grow without really wanting to. The rhythm of life changes, and it often takes us a while to get the new beat down. We go like gangbusters for years and years, then wake up one day and find that our old enthusiasms have been extinguished. Or that we have a sudden urgency to pursue long-suppressed dreams, or things we've never even thought of before.

The conventional view of growth places a big emphasis on intention. You decide how you want to grow. You then set goals, create an execution plan, and finally get down to work. You follow a *program*. This conventional view makes sense; after all, it's pretty much how most professional people went through school and the early years of their careers.

However, this is not the full picture.

Growth is often messy. Growth depends partly on what's going on within you, and partly on what's going on in the world around you.

When my clients consider the future, rarely is the right direction obvious. Usually there are multiple possible directions. Each one is a bit enticing. And each presents huge uncertainties.

For example, I really want to be a talk show host. And I really want to be a crack political operative. And I really want to write the seminal novel of our time. And I really want to start an international nonprofit that will build and support schools for poor children in developing countries. And I wouldn't mind moving to a college town in the Midwest and becoming the local dynamo running the civic light opera. Meanwhile, I have this coaching business that I'm interested in taking up a few notches.

I can see these visions pretty clearly. They are glittery and fascinating. And I can also see that I can't do them all—certainly not at once. I also see that if I try to do them all, I may not do any of them. So what do I do?

The answer is experimentation.

How Career Experimentation Works

Experimentation is the way we check out how well our ideas correspond to reality. Experimentation stimulates new thinking. It makes new avenues possible. It protects us from running pell-mell into things that aren't going to be suitable for us.

Remember the famous politician from chapter 3? He needed to do some experimentation. What he needed to figure out couldn't be worked out just by thinking.

A key source for understanding how this works is Herminia Ibarra's *Working Identity*. Ibarra, formerly a professor at Harvard Business School and now at INSEAD outside Paris, addresses the question of how career change actually works, as opposed to how people think it *should*

123

work. "Conventional wisdom," she writes, "tells us that the key to making a successful change lies in first *knowing*—with as much clarity and certainty as possible—what we really want to do and then using that knowledge to implement a sound strategy."

Ibarra continues: "But career change doesn't follow the conventional method. We learn who we are—in practice, not theory—by testing reality, not by looking inside. We discover the true possibilities by *doing*—trying out new activities, reaching out to new groups, finding new role models, and reworking our story as we tell it to those around us."

Experimenting is trying on an outfit before you buy it. It's inhabiting a role to see what it's like. It's testing a hypothesis to see if it flies. It's seeing how your feelings line up with your thoughts.

When you experiment, you experience, check things out, vet, discuss, test, and mix things up. The information you get allows you to reconfigure, reshape, and experiment again. A good experiment is something bigger than a casual stab and something less than a wholesale repackaging of your life.

Taking a class is an experiment. Reading a book on something new is an experiment. Having an informational interview or going on a real interview is an experiment. Attending a conference or convention outside your normal area is an experiment. Taking a trip is an experiment. Hanging out with people in a different field is an experiment. Trying your hand at a new type of work is an experiment. Volunteering is an experiment. Serving as an advisor to a start-up is an experiment. Joining a board is an experiment.

Examples of Experiments

- Reading a book or article on a new subject
- Having an informal conversation with a friend
- Going on an informational interview
- Going on a job interview
- Giving a job talk
- Shadowing a job for a day
- Taking a class
- Attending a conference
- Going to a professional event
- Writing an article
- Crafting a new positioning statement
- Hosting a dinner party for people who reflect your new interests
- Developing a business plan
- Advising an organization or company
- Volunteering
- Being a consultant
- Serving on a board or committee
- Hiring a consultant
- Traveling

Exercise: Brainstorm Experiments

Consider some of the goals you have. They may be related to professional development, changing careers, or another area of interest. Write down five potential experiments related to one of your goals.

Goal: _____

Experiments:

1. _____

2. _____

3. _____

4. _____

5. _____

(If you find this exercise difficult, try doing the "Designing Career Experiments" exercise at the end of the chapter as a way of stimulating additional thoughts.)

Experimenting *Enough*

Ibarra refers to the process of experimentation as "committed flirtation." It's continuing to check out a path without being sure it is for you. In a statistics sense, it is collecting enough data to make a reasonable conclusion.

Most professionals get the idea of experimentation. However, *they typically don't go deep enough.* They abandon the experiment too early.

At the time Sanjay Lal took one of my workshops, he had been out on his own for several months after working as an attorney for about five years. Sanjay was discouraged. He had left his career in order to do something more creative, either in writing or film/video production, but nothing good had emerged.

"I've tried a lot of things," he said, "but nothing seems to have worked out so for. I've done a lot of networking, taken a class, tried my hand at writing, but things don't seem to be going anywhere."

I asked him about his writing.

"I tried writing full-time. I would go to Starbucks every day and write. But it hasn't led to anything. Maybe it's not for me."

"How long did you do you this?" I asked.

"I guess around three weeks," he replied.

Most of Sanjay's other experiments were similarly short. He'd identified decent experiments; he just hadn't done anything in depth.

"How long did you practice law?" I asked.

"Five years."

"And how long were you in law school?"

"Three years."

"Did you clerk, or work as a paralegal?"

"I clerked for a year."

"So," I calculated, "You've spent around nine years pursuing one career, that you don't particularly like . . ."

"I think I see your point," he said.

"And how long have you been actively seeking something else?"

"For about four months. Actually, less, because my wife and I took a three-week honeymoon at first."

The moral of this story? Sanjay had invested nine years building a legal career. His decision to leave law was based on a great deal of evidence. He knew a lot about being a lawyer and about how he himself responded to the requirements and opportunities of the profession.

However, four months of exploration amounted to little more than a cursory overview of a few alternatives. It was better than nothing, but it wasn't nearly enough time. What he needed was to devise meaningful experiments, experience alternatives deeply, develop a network, reshape ideas, and begin to build something different.

If you compare something in which you've invested nine years of your life against something in which you've invested a lot less, you are dooming your new alternative to failure. It can't measure up. You need to strengthen it before you can judge it.

At the time we first met, I sensed that Sanjay didn't really want to make additional investments of time, effort, and foregone income. He had given up a lot already. He wanted a path with a clear goal, and he wanted assurance that continued efforts toward that goal would yield success.

But he didn't have any of those things. Not yet, anyway. He had to stay the course without quite knowing where the course would lead him.

Deepening Experiments

Experimenting is an art. It requires you to *deepen* your experiments at the same time that you find ways to make them *efficient*.

Deepening means intensifying, focusing, or repeating what you're doing. It also means getting out of the shallow end of the pool and opening yourself up to uncertainty or discomfort.

Recall how Bridget O'Callaghan, the lawyer/jeweler, gradually deepened her experiments. She took one class, then another. She designed pieces and sold them first to her friends and then to a retail store. She attended trade shows. She set up a website. Each of these experiments gave her additional information about what worked, what she liked, and what additional challenges she faced.

Consider some additional examples of ways to deepen experiments.

The Experimenters' Journeys

For about two years, Bridget O'Callaghan explored different ways of reformatting her life. There were no big breakthroughs, but things started shifting.

SIMPLE EXPERIMENT	DEEPENED EXPERIMENT
• Being an occasional advisor to a start-up	• Working with one of the founders to rewrite the business plan and participating in a presentation to potential investors
• Joining a city bar committee on a new area of law or policy—say, equal opportunity	• Serving as the point person to line up speakers for an upcoming symposium
• Making a first trip to China to see its art and architecture	• Spending two days hanging out in galleries and studios in Shanghai; figuring out their business model

She continued designing and selling jewelry, but cut down on the number of shows she was attending. Pulling back from sales allowed her to think more about strategy.

Through networking, Bridget met a small-business expert, Stefaan Marien, who sat down with her for several hours and helped her see where she was in terms of small-business development and what a reasonable time frame for growth might be. This reduced the number of issues she had to worry about, since it turned out that she would not need to reach some decisions for quite some time.

The departure of two other lawyers gave her more power vis-à-vis her mercurial boss, and she used it to demand more regular hours and greater support. Bridget's husband, who had experienced his own career angst, got a great job. And she got pregnant.

For now, Bridget is going to let her jewelry business develop at a controlled tempo. It's too early to know whether it could be the next big thing or is better as a very satisfying form of creative expression. Perhaps the larger shift is that she doesn't feel that her jewelry business needs to save her. Her work situation is tolerable now. Not great, but not toxic either.

"I'm a lot more into letting things unfold at their own pace, rather than waiting for some perfect result," she says. "While I'm not sure when great things will happen to me, I know they will. For now, I'm happy where I'm at."

Sanjay Lal also progressed.

Sanjay, like many lawyers, turned out to be a dutiful student. So even though he didn't really *want* to go back to experimenting (and the related tasks like networking and honing his communications), he did as instructed.

A few months later, Sanjay was working full-time for a video production company. He'd made the first big transition—albeit from volunteer labor to low-paid labor. But he was *in*. He had a foothold in a new world and a sense of strategy for how he would march forward. His experiments had another important result: they redoubled his interest in video production.

"I feel like I know now how to access the world," he said. "It's exciting. I feel awake again."

ADDITIONAL EXERCISES

Exercise: Designing Career Experiments

An experiment is anything that gives you new information about a career or life alternative. You don't need a grand passion to justify an experiment—anything that elicits a twinge, inkling, or interest is worth exploring.

As rapidly as you can, write responses to the following prompts:

1. A class I'd like to attend: _____
2. A subject I'd like to read more about: _____
3. A place in the U.S. I'd like to visit: _____
4. A place overseas I'd like to visit: _____
5. A job I'd like to shadow for a day: _____
6. A stranger I'd like to meet: _____
7. A skill I could offer as a volunteer or advisor: _____
8. A place I could volunteer: _____
9. An ordinary person I'd like to interview: _____
10. A famous person I'd like to interview: _____
11. An environment I'd like to spend two days in: _____
12. A company I'd like to hang out at for one day: _____
13. A skill I'd like to develop: _____
14. A conference I'd like to attend: _____
15. A person I'd like to get to know better: _____

Circle the response above that is the hardest to do, or least likely to happen. Brainstorm with someone about ways you could explore this topic.

Exercise: Field Trips

This exercise is to plan and take several field trips. Field trips are all about experiential learning. These are closer to play than work. In a well-executed field trip, there's nothing to prepare or memorize—you just see, hear, touch, smell, taste, and experience. They may lead to something you are explicitly searching for, or to something unexpected. Some ideas for field trips include:

1. Check out an inexpensive play, dance performance, or concert.
2. Take a twenty dollar bill and spend it on magazines that are fun to hold and read.

129

3. Do some armchair traveling—plan a weeklong trip to someplace exotic (or someplace so prosaic it seems exotic).

4. Sample a free class at the Apple Store.

5. Sample a free class at Home Depot.

Now add some ideas of your own:

1. _____

2. _____

3. _____

4. _____

5. _____

6. _____

7. _____

8. _____

9. _____

10. _____

READING LIST

Herminia Ibarra, *Working Identity*

The best book for professionals on career transition, bar none. Ibarra, a professor at INSEAD, conducted the research for this book when she was a professor at Harvard Business School. She sees career transition as an evolving process involving experimentation, new connections, and making sense. The great takeaway from her book is that a major part of moving forward is acting before you are ready to act, engaging in a process of "committed flirtation" whereby you take action based on certain goals but open yourself up to the serendipity of what will actually happen.

Fredric Hudson, *The Adult Years*

Hudson's theories for how growth occurs have been an important resource for me in both my coaching and my own life. Hudson is the founder of the Hudson Institute of Santa Barbara, where I received my coaching certification. This book sets forth his core models. Complex and highly illuminating.

CHAPTER 12

Learning Inside and Outside the Job

Let's say you've reached the top. You've made it, by all conventional criteria. Does that mean that you can coast? Get by on what you know already?

Not really. Take Ralph Baxter, for instance.

In the early 1990s, Ralph became the chairman and CEO of Orrick Herrington & Sutcliffe, LLP. His job includes devising strategy, monitoring results, and building the management team that runs the firm. Most firms are headed by managing partners who continue to practice law. Ralph doesn't practice law. He flies around the world, managing and leading the firm.

Ralph's promotion to chairman and CEO was based partly on his being a partner and respected lawyer already. However, his legal background provided only some of the competencies he would need to do his job well. He had run the firm's labor department and had taken leadership positions in his schooling days. But before he became chairman, nothing he'd done had been on such a large scale.

"I really didn't know if I had the skill set to be leader of the law firm," he said. "I thought I was as well suited as anybody who was being considered, but that didn't mean I was good enough."

How did Ralph deal with this situation? For one thing, by recognizing what he didn't know. "I had the self-awareness that the job was going to require me to do different things than the things that I'd been trained to do."

Ralph basically created an on-the-job learning plan for himself. "I tried to pay attention," he said. "I hired consultants to help me, and I read." He took formal study where it existed, such as enrolling in a program through Harvard Business School on professional service firm leadership and management. His classmates came from consulting, architecture, and accounting, as well as law.

What didn't already exist, he created. Ralph initiated the Law Firm Leaders Forum, now in its twelfth year, which is a seminar for leaders from major law firms around the world to talk about issues and solutions. "I created that in part because there wasn't anyplace for me to go and sit down with others who were struggling with the same things."

Developing the competencies to lead a major firm required sustained effort.

"It takes a lot of work," Ralph says. "It's a different skill set. So we know we have to learn."

One might see Ralph Baxter's experience as apocryphal. In fact, it's illustrative of what nearly all professionals experience as their careers progress. Professional growth requires constant learning—not simply because it is required to keep up but also because learning is what keeps work interesting and fulfilling.

Learning is more likely to occur if you plan for it. And while it's important to plan how you can keep learning *within* your job, it's also important to consider ways of learning *outside of* your job—what I call "parallel growth."

Learning and Professional Satisfaction

It's hard to be happy if you don't know what you're doing. And it's hard to be happy if what you are doing is so familiar that it's boring.

Psychologist Mihalyi Csikszentmihalyi, who developed the groundbreaking concept of "flow," shows how these two ideas are related. "Flow," a feeling of deep engagement and fulfillment, arises when three things are present:

1. You are dealing with a high level of challenge.
2. Your level of skill matches the challenge.
3. You experience constant feedback.

As an illustration, think of skiing. If you're coasting down low-grade beginner slopes, it might be too easy. It's boring. On the other hand, if you're hurtling down knee-destroying moguls, you might find it too difficult. It becomes frustrating. The place where you feel most invigorated is when you are just at the edge of what you can do, but not beyond it. This is when you become so absorbed in the experience that you lose track of time. And when you reach the bottom of the mountain, you want to go right back up. That's *flow*.

Flow lasts only if you keep the challenge level high; otherwise, it sinks into boredom. Often, however, there is a transition period when new work requires skills that are not sufficiently developed. At these points, work may become frustrating—for a time. But if you keep developing skills, some of the most frustrating situations can end up being highly fulfilling.

Exercise: What I'd Like to Learn

Quickly write down five things you'd like to learn in the future, just for the sake of learning them. Some examples might include learning to speak Portuguese, how to water ski, or how to mount a spare tire.

1. _____
2. _____
3. _____
4. _____
5. _____

Articulating Competencies

Competencies are the building blocks of performance. They are the skills, knowledge, and traits that enable you to get things done. Any task in life calls for certain competencies, whether that task is writing a will, building a supercollider, or cooking Veal Prince Orloff. Competencies are what you bring to the table. Table 12-1 shows a few examples.

In the professional world, we tend to think of "résumés" and "experience" when evaluating our qualifications. But your experiences and formal credentials are just proxies for what you know how to do.

When you are being interviewed for a job, an employer—whether she knows it or not—is evaluating your competencies. If you lead with your competencies rather than your work history, you are able to guide the potential employer into understanding your actual value. This is particularly useful when you are making a career change, since your past jobs may not match a potential employer's preconceived notion of the ideal candidate's work history. By articulating your competencies up front, you directly address the issue of what you can offer, rather than leaving it open to interpretation.

TABLE 12-1. EXAMPLES OF COMPETENCIES

Skills	Knowledge	Traits
• Leadership	• Players in the	• Hard-working
• Market research	New York media	• Enthusiastic
• Legal analysis	market	• Creative
• Software coding	• Structure of the	• Ethical
• Project	Argentine grocery	• Calm in a crisis
management	sector	• Organized
• Writing and	• The '40 Act	• Detail-oriented
editing	• Multicultural	
• Media buying	communication	
• Sales	• Drug-company	
• Classroom	testing regimens	
management	• Needlepoint	
• CPR	techniques	

Similarly, when a client asks you to tell him about your past work in a field, what he is really saying is, "Explain to me how you can help me solve my problem." The more directly you articulate your competencies, the more likely you are to convince him of your capabilities.

Well-managed organizations evaluate performance on the basis of specific, clearly articulated competencies that are identified ahead of time. Professional services firms are just now getting into this line of thinking; traditionally people in these organizations have been promoted for technical rather than managerial skills.

Legal organizations have also begun incorporating competency models into their training, review, and promotion processes. What is interesting about these models is how much the desired competencies for high-performing lawyers are not purely or specifically "legal" but instead relate to more general characteristics such as maturity, leadership, client skills, communication, self-motivation, and work management.

Assessing Competency Gaps

What competencies do you need to develop in order to move ahead?

As an example, consider Mona, a litigator and government attorney who would like to move into arts management. Some of Mona's competencies relate to the work of being a lawyer, and others arise from her personality and her long-standing support of arts organizations.

She is a natural organizer and networker and has high emotional intelligence. She knows how to get things going. In the future, she wants to learn the nuts and bolts of running arts organizations so she can offer actual knowledge rather than pure instinct. She also wants to balance her relationship-building skills with the ability not to take things personally. Here is how her current and desired competencies differ:

MONA'S COMPETENCY GAP ANALYSIS

Current competencies	*Desired competencies*
• Legal analysis • Writing and editing • Organizational skills • International/Multicultural • Networking • Managerial acumen	**Legal:** Better procedural skills; client management **Managerial:** Accounting, operations, reporting to board **Arts:** Experience with organizations

Exercise: Competency Gap Analysis

Consider how your career will develop in the next few years. Describe the competencies you have as well as those you need to acquire.

COMPETENCY GAP ANALYSIS

Current competencies	*Desired competencies*
1. _____	1. _____
2. _____	2. _____
3. _____	3. _____
4. _____	4. _____
5. _____	5. _____

MP

Master Plan Intervention!

Copy your Competency Gap Analysis over to the blank Master Plan template in the appendix.

Box 12-1. Special Competencies

The following are some competencies that are rarely spoken about but are, in my view, crucial to long-term success.

Conveying a sense of specialization, while being a capable generalist. As you rise in your career, you will be expected by employers and clients to offer a certain type of specialized skill. (As one of my clients put it, "You want to be known as the person who does the thing.") At the same time, actual success in getting things done requires strong generalist talents: organizational skills, resourcefulness, good communications, solid emotional intelligence, and so forth. In essence, you need to market specialized skills while building generalized skills.

Back-office skills. Much of the success of small businesses is built on back-office functions such as accounting, inventory management, collections, IT systems, physical maintenance, and tax and regulatory compliance. This is true whether you're selling high-end handbags or immigration services. If you are running your own operation, you need to educate yourself about these functions and ideally find people who are capable of managing them.

Making yourself essential. One lawyer told me, "My main task is to make it extremely painful for my bosses to do without me." The more essential you make yourself to your clients, your organization, or your direct superiors, the stronger a position you will be in. However, keep in mind that the nature of this *changes over time.* The same lawyer adds: "When I started working, it was enough that I was a capable, smart, industrious attorney who was somewhat cheaper than the market rate. But I have to up my game, because in a few years I don't want them thinking that they could replace me with someone similar to who I used to be, at a lower salary. So now I'm shifting my focus to being more relevant from a business development perspective."

Establishing a Professional Learning Plan

You might luck out and find a great mentor or colleague who takes it upon herself to bring you along. Or perhaps the institution you work for has a solid training program that responds to your needs as they arise.

But honestly? You will be much better off if you assume stewardship of your own learning. Assess what you need to know, figure out where you can get it, and go after it. The world is more likely to offer you resources if you've thought about the kinds of resources you need.

Exercise: The Ingredients of Your Professional Learning Plan

After reviewing your desired future competencies, write answers to the following questions. (See box 12-2 for an example.)

1. What kind of formal training exists?

2. What kind of experiences will educate me?

3. Who would be a good mentor?

4. Who can help me in other ways?

5. How can I get honest feedback?

6. What's a reasonable time frame to achieve this?

Box 12-2. Example: George's Professional Learning Plan

George, the junior associate in structured finance from chapter 1, focused part of his Professional Learning Plan on the competencies he would need in the future related to running a business. Although he didn't expect this to happen for several years, he wanted to begin building the foundation even as he continued developing his legal skills.

1. *What kind of formal training exists?*
   Classes exist in various aspects of starting and running a business. An MBA would be useful, but is not something I want to do.

2. *What kind of experiences will educate me?*
   Since I am interested in an import business (at least now), the best experiences would be small-scale efforts at importing and selling different products. I might also be able to get involved with friends who are entrepreneurs, adding value in some way to be determined. In addition, I could attend an imported products convention, just to see what the world is like.

3. *Who would be a good mentor?*
   The ideal mentor would be (1) someone who has worked in law or consulting and then started an entrepreneurial effort or (2) someone who has done it all on their own (basically, a entrepreneur without an MBA—like an early Steve Jobs!).

4. *Who can help me in other ways?*
   Since my ideas are still undeveloped, anyone who can offer ideas, perspectives, or connections to the entrepreneurial world would be helpful. It would also be good for me to get to know rich lawyers and businesspeople, in case I eventually want outside investors.

5. *How can I get honest feedback?*
   The most meaningful feedback I can get is by actually trying different things. Since most people I work with do not have the same interests I do, it would probably be a good idea to avoid getting feedback from them on this particular goal.

6. *What's a reasonable time frame to achieve this?*
   It will be at least five years before I have the financial security to do something like this. However, I could easily start testing out small possibilities right now, such as trying to resell the Vietnamese lacquerware I loaded up on during our honeymoon. EBay Powerselling, here I come!

Growth outside the Job: Jennifer and the Dolphins

Sometimes the most significant growth is the kind that takes places outside of the job.

Jennifer Powell and I both attended the coaching certification program of the Hudson Institute of Santa Barbara. An energetic, animated, can-do person, she had spent than two decades working in Corporate America. She was on track to retire from a major insurance company in the Northeast, but had no intention from retiring from working. There were a lot of things she wanted to do with her life.

One of these was to work with dolphins. Her dream was to get a job working full time with dolphins following her retirement. This was one of the first things I learned about her, and I got the impression it was one of the first things that anyone learned about her. She was open and shameless about her passion.

Our coaching program consisted of several long weekends over the course of a year, so the members of our small group got to know each other better. At each meeting, Jennifer included an update on her dolphin plans. She was making contact with researchers in Florida. She was spending part of her spring vacation volunteering at a dolphin research institute. She was looking at real estate in Florida.

"That's great!" we all exclaimed, supportively. But I couldn't tell whether we thought it was great that she was getting close to her goal, or just that she was trying. We all graduated and went our separate ways.

A few months ago, our group received an email update from Jennifer. She had moved to Florida and had semiretired from her company—she was still working twenty hours a week doing chief of staff duties. She was building her coaching business.

And she was working full-time in the education department of the Dolphin Research Center in Florida, conducting workshops and narrating sessions with the dolphins and their trainers. "I love it and am living my dream!!!" she wrote.

So there you go. Jennifer Powell did it. To me, her accomplishment is amazing. It seems way harder than starting a company or going back to graduate school or selling a screenplay.

Jennifer Powell's dream became real because she kept at it. Over time, she *made herself* into the perfect dolphin institute employee.

Jennifer undertook a process of what I call "parallel growth." She pursued more than one major objective at the same time. In fact, she pursued three: maintaining a high-level position at a major corporation; pursuing coaching training and building a coaching practice; and making work with dolphins a part of her life. She didn't necessarily invest in each of these the same amount of time, money, or energy, but she made each a priority. That's parallel growth.

The Benefits of Parallel Growth

Parallel growth means taking meaningful action toward different goals. As you develop your legal career, you should also be developing things that are important to you that may have little or nothing to do with your legal career. Your current job or specialty will get the majority of your attention. It's probably your most marketable skill. But you can start laying the groundwork for your other interests, whether professional or personal. You can explore broadly, learn deeply, build a network, develop credibility, and prepare to enter another endeavor at a level of competence and comfort at a later stage.

Parallel growth, done well, means that when you are ready to let go of your trapeze bar, another one is gracefully swinging toward you at just the right time.

Growing one or more interests in parallel has a number of advantages. First, it provides *balance*. The more you cultivate an interest—whether it's running marathons, writing children's books, investing in real estate, or learning to sea-kayak—the more it stands on its own and carves out space against the demands of your job.

Second, it leads to *meaningful engagement*. Feelings of flow, or peak experience, are much more likely to come from activities where you have broad knowledge or deep expertise. The more established these pursuits are, the more easily you can step into them and experience optimal engagement.

Third, parallel growth creates the possibility of *positive career development or transitions*. It allows you the chance to develop expertise in an area without being judged for your performance in it. Then, when you decide to make a switch, you already have several years of experience, as well as an extensive network. You talk the lingo, can activate a relevant network, and know the tradeoffs. Often, when people appear to have made sudden shifts in jobs or fields, the reality is that the switch has not been so sudden. It's been prepared over a number of years, during which time the individual has had time to learn, reflect, network, and plan. Parallel growth can help you experience a smooth transition instead of a cold awakening.

Fourth, it *takes a lot of stress out of your life*. When you accept that it doesn't all have to happen in one career, you free yourself to enjoy what you have without making unrealistic demands on it. And when you find parallel interests to engage in, you stop floating around in a miasma of unfocused energy. You stop thinking and start doing, and in doing, you may find answers to many of your own persistent questions.

Sometimes parallel growth leads to lives where you are actually doing more than one career simultaneously. Marci Alboher has written of this phenomenon in her book, *One Person/Multiple Careers: How the Slash Effect Can Work for You*. She gives scores of examples of people who have combined careers in attractive, compelling, and workable ways—a psychiatrist/violinmaker, a football player/lawyer/television host, an art consultant/Pilates teacher, and so on. One of the points of her book is that this is desirable, not simply something to manage. Creating a "slash" career can be a way to accept our own complexity rather than trying to stuff ourselves into a single box with a simple label.

Other times, parallel growth ends up making our core career more satisfying and effective. Shortly after she switched from public-interest work to the private sector, Chris Palamountain became a commissioner on the San Francisco Redevelopment Commission, a powerful and prestigious position. People assume that her work as a lawyer created the foundation for this role. In fact, the opposite was true. Her public policy interests developed separately from her legal work, but her experiences on the Redevelopment Commission have improved her persuasive, political, and business skills.

Exercise: Brainstorm Methods of Parallel Growth

Consider an interest you have outside the parameters of your job. Write a few sentences on what you could do over the next several years to make this a significant part of your life.

_____

_____

_____

_____

_____

_____

MP

Master Plan Intervention!

Copy your parallel growth goals over to the Master Plan template in the appendix. List experiments that can help you with either those goals or your general professional learning.

READING LIST

Marci Alboher, *One Person/Multiple Careers: How the Slash Effect Can Work for You*

Alboher, a lawyer turned writer, has come up with a new framework for viewing careers that offers freedom, creativity, and power. Her theory is that the "slash" concept for describing oneself (think "actor-slash-model," etc.) extends far beyond the realm of aspiring creative types with humdrum day jobs. She runs through a fascinating number of unlikely but convincingly integrated "slash" professionals. Alboher's point is that slash careers are not things to explain away—they are things to aspire to. Her book is filled with practical recommendations on how to launch, manage, and balance slash careers.

Biographies can also be a great resource for continued learning. I asked Sayuri Rajapakse, a lawyer in New Jersey who is one of my favorite book recommenders, for some of her top picks. Here they are:

Letitia Baldridge, *A Lady, First*

Known to the public primarily as Jacqueline Kennedy's spinster chief of staff, Baldridge carved out a career as a diplomat, business executive, politico, entrepreneur, wife, parent, and best-selling author of several books. A fascinating account of a woman who, lacking beauty, wealth, and any clear guidance on how to succeed in a male-dominated world, managed to create a thrilling and meaningful life for herself.

Richard Branson, *Losing My Virginity*

Branson's autobiography portrays the rise of a man whose primary goal in life has been to have fun. The founder of Virgin Records and Virgin Atlantic, he is the rare media figure who seems as interesting as the hype. The book works both as a rollicking, witty read and as a business thriller. Branson's school headmaster once predicted that he would either go to prison or become a millionaire; this book shows that the two alternatives are not so far removed from one other.

Grace Mirabella, *In and Out of Vogue*

After Diana Vreeland and before Anna Wintour, Grace Mirabella ran *Vogue*. Her autobiography is an interesting story of how a girl from an Italian immigrant family in Newark, New Jersey, succeeded in joining the in-crowd and then rose above it. Along with Letitia Baldridge and Katharine Graham, she is an example of someone who carved out a life for herself against family and social expectations, figuring out what was necessary to survive and triumph in a dog-eat-dog world.

M. M. Kaye, *Enchanted Evening*

Kaye, the author of such sprawling historical fiction as *The Far Pavilions*, spent the early decades of her life in India, China, and Japan during the declining years of the British Empire. Her several volumes of autobiography (*Enchanted Evening* is the third) are rich with detailed observations not only of that world but also of the more universal themes of love and loss.

CHAPTER 13

Money and Other Blocks

Here's a definition of being stuck: It's when you can't change things, but at the same time can't accept the way things are.

When you are stuck, you don't see any viable alternatives to the present situation. There is just that one, problematic reality. There is no away around it. Or so it appears.

One way to deal with being stuck is to explore the alternatives that are *not* on the table. These are the options that do not *seem* like viable options. This method of getting unstuck requires you to listen to what's *not* being said. It may require you to interrogate your taboos.

At this point in history, we are pretty open about discussing most things. However, in the context of career development and career change, there are a handful of options that are sometimes considered taboo. As soon as they are mentioned, inquiry ceases—you don't want to go down that road. In this manner, otherwise legitimate preferences end up blocking progress. These include:

- Money
- Status
- Lifestyle
- Geography
- Starting over

To these, I would add two situations that are not exactly taboos, but nonetheless tend to stymie progress:

- Choosing a small change when a larger one is called for
- Avoiding a small change when a larger one is not possible

This chapter is about the way these issues can block progress, and what to do about them.

Money as a Distraction

Money affects what you can do with your life. However, it operates differently from the way most people think.

In coaching, I have observed that people tend to talk about money in the same way regardless of their actual financial status. Often they use exactly the same words.

Here's what I mean: If you ask professional people how much they need to earn to be satisfied, they'll typically name a number higher than what they now earn. This is true whether they make $20,000 per year, $200,000 per year, or $2,000,000 per year. If they are very wealthy, they may say that continuing to earn the same amount will be sufficient, but it is the rare client indeed who believes that he or she could get by while earning less. Note that I'm not asking these clients, "Could you be fulfilled with less money?" I'm asking them, "Could you *get by* with less money?"

Similarly, if you ask people what is stopping them from making particular changes in their lives that they are really keen on making, they will usually offer money as a primary reason.

Clearly, money has significant psychological uses apart from fulfilling actual material needs. It can be a way of keeping score, being recognized, and earning validation. It's a source of security, identity, and comfort. Money is an indicator of status. It can create power and weakness in relationships.

What is relevant for us is how money can be a *distraction* in the process of changing your life—in other words, how it can keep you stuck. Money can prevent change and hinder personal development when:

- you allow concerns about future income to stop you from exploring interesting alternatives
- you base future actions primarily on sunk costs
- you allow money to be a consolation prize for not living other important values
- you are not conscious of the amounts of money you earn, spend, and save

Let's explore these situations in more detail.

When Money Impedes Exploration

I often ask clients to describe the different future options they find interesting. Usually, as soon as they start talking about those alternative visions, they start mentioning the financial barriers to these options: "But the salaries in that sector are really low," "But I couldn't live on that," "But everyone knows most new businesses fail." They do this without being prompted. Evaluating things in terms of their financial payoff appears to be a built-in reflex.

The problem is that prematurely thinking about money usually short-circuits the process of exploration. Without an intervention, the client will continue down the path of identifying problems and barriers and then dismissing an alternative as nonviable without exploring it. The inquiry ends before it begins.

This is not good. Why? Because the first vision, the one that is being held to the harsh metrics of financial merit, is only one version of how things might turn out. At the beginning of any exploration, there are countless unknowns.

Imagine, for example, that an experienced lawyer currently earning $125,000 a year articulates a vision of working for a nonprofit organization focused on schools. The actual manifestation of this vision could be one of many things. For instance, she could end up as a full-time employee of a nonprofit organization, earning between one-third and one-half of her former salary. Or she could serve as a member of the board of directors of an innovative school-reform organization while continuing to work as a lawyer. Or she might become an influential supporter of a charter school, decide to raise money to build a school in a developing country, or start shifting her practice so that she spends more time on public policy, legislative, and lobbying matters. It's also possible that, as she gets in touch with what's really important to her, her own sense of the importance of money vis-à-vis other values will change and things that formerly seemed impossible will seem not just possible but easy choices. Perhaps in the end she will leave law and become an educator. Who knows what might happen?

The point is that she will likely do *none* of these things if she concludes at the beginning of the process that her vision won't pay enough, because then she won't even bother exploring.

When you are contemplating interesting future visions, take money off the table for a while. You can address it later, when you have a more robust set of choices.

When Future Actions Are Based on Sunk Costs

A *sunk cost*, you will recall from economics class, is a cost you have already incurred. There is no way to get it back. For example, your law school tuition, or the years you spent in a bad relationship. Oy!

Economics teaches that you should not base decisions on sunk costs. What's done is done. Instead, you should look objectively at potential future returns.

Sunk costs as a distraction shows up in career coaching when people say things like, "I don't like being a civil litigator, but I've put all this time and money into it, so I guess I should make something out of it." Or, "This novel isn't going anywhere, but I've spent four years working on it, so I can't just give it up."

It's appropriate to look at the *assets* you have—whether they consist of a legal education or a novel in progress—when examining your future prospects. But the fact that you've spent a lot of time doing something is, by itself, irrelevant.

A corollary to not making decisions based on sunk costs is to be aware that everything has an *opportunity cost*. If you do one thing, you will *not* be doing something else. So if you continue working in a field that is not satisfying to you, you will *not* be building expertise in another area that might be more interesting. If you continue writing a novel you hate, you may be preventing yourself from writing one you love.

When thinking about money, focus on the future, not the past.

When Money Serves as a Consolation Prize

A consolation prize is what contestants receive when they don't actually win. The sponsors don't want them to go home empty-handed. You've been great, have a safe trip home, enjoy this lovely tote bag.

Sometimes, high salaries are a consolation prize for not having a job or life that you like. So you take expensive three-day ski weekends instead of developing a sense of fulfillment. You receive an end-of-year bonus in exchange for successive all-nighters that have endangered your physical and mental health.

You can give out consolation prizes, too—expensive gifts for loved ones who don't get much of your time. You can allow yourself some shopping therapy as partial compensation for all the stress.

Earning a lot of money can mask a state of profound values dissatisfaction. A high income brings a lot social approbation. People may not like you, but they assume that you have it made. They are sure that if they had your high salary, life would be wonderful.

Money is a problem when it prevents you from investigating what your values actually are. You get stuck if you avoid looking deeper and yet cannot satisfy yourself with the way things are. The Wizard's voice orders you to ignore the man behind the curtain, but you can't help peeking over.

150

If you find that you are trying to convince yourself that you have a great life when in fact you experience a continual, gnawing discomfort, you may need to make a concerted effort to get in touch with your actual values. (Try the exercises in chapter 3, as well as some of the books recommended in that chapter, for some ways to do this.) If the people around you cannot connect with what you believe to be your actual values, start associating with people who do. Reconnect with people who knew you before you made the big bucks, or who know you for other attributes.

When You're Not Conscious of How You Use Money

I worked as an associate for several years for Davis Polk & Wardwell in New York. When I started working for the firm, many of the first-year attorneys, myself included, had large amounts of law school debt. A lot of them ended up going further into debt during their first year of work. This was odd, given that, at the time, Davis Polk was tied for offering the highest law firm salaries in the country.

How could something like this happen? Because some of my colleagues were simply not conscious of how much it cost to live in Manhattan. Since they were getting salaries that were high by any rational criteria, higher than anything they'd ever earned before, they assumed they didn't really have to keep track of the details. As a result, they spent more than they earned—which is easy to do in Manhattan, I can assure you.

If you are not conscious of how you earn, spend, or save money, you are in its grip. It's hard to make forward progress when a significant part of your life is unknown territory. Getting conscious requires you to collect data about what is really going on in your financial life and to examine some of the reasons you behave the way you do around money.

I find that many people, including me, resist this process. What we *really* want is to have enough money so that we don't have to think about it. However, unless you have assets of, say, a hundred million dollars or more, you can't really get around the need to be conscious of the way you use money. Otherwise, your career decisions will be warped by unknowns and unresolved issues.

Exercise: Money Consciousness Quiz

1. What is your approximate net worth?

2. Do you currently carry credit card debt? If so, why?

3. If you have credit card debt, when do you plan to pay it off fully?

4. Do you have outstanding school loans? If so, how many years has it been since you graduated?

5. How much did you spend at restaurants in the past month?

6. How much per year do you spend at Starbucks (or your other favorite coffeehouse)?

7. The last time you shopped for clothes, how much did you spend?

8. How much have you saved for retirement?

9. If you do not own a house or apartment, in what year do you expect to buy one?

10. In the past five years, have you borrowed money or requested financial gifts from a relative? If so, why?

Were these questions easy for you to answer? If they weren't, what kind of emotions did they provoke? What do your answers say about how *conscious* you are about how you use and spend money?

When you are not entirely conscious of how you use money, taking the first step—figuring out exactly what is going on—can be very difficult. The resistance that has led us to this place shows up in full force. But once you get clear about what's going on, it's not that difficult to take specific steps to improve things. In some ways, following a financial plan is actually easier than creating one.

Exercise: Hire a Financial Planner

If you don't have a financial plan already, hire a financial planner. I prefer financial planners who are fee-based rather than those who are paid according to assets under management—my goal is disinterested advice.

Going through the process of financial planning forces you to get real about the place of money in your life.

Exercise: Experience a Money-Limited Day

Remove all your bank cards and credit cards from your wallet or purse. Leave yourself just ten or twenty dollars—whatever you reasonably think is necessary to get through the day. Then go about your normal activities.

As you go through your day, notice what kinds of emotions you experience. What is it like not to be living in a constant state of potential expenditure?

Other Blocks That Inhibit Progress

Money is not the only block. Other things can also block progress. See whether you recognize yourself in any of the following scenarios.

Status

Dora, an auditor with a major accounting firm, wants to work more directly with people rather than with data. She has a strong interest in entering the coaching profession, but she is concerned about how it would look. "I like working with people, but I don't want to go to one of those random coaching training programs. They seem so cheesy. And I think I would feel weird calling myself a coach."

Lifestyle

Janet, a consultant, and her husband, a banker, have been unemployed for several months as a result of nearly simultaneous layoffs. Both are ambivalent about returning to the fields they left, partly because of the tremendous stress of their jobs. Their expenses are more than $20,000 per month. However, they don't want to downsize, and they resist cutting back on their expenditures. "We really love our house and the area, and the public schools are not nearly as good as the private ones."

Geography

Jonathan is an intellectual property lawyer who has lived in Denver since graduating from law school six years ago. Denver salaries are relatively low, in part because of the large number of people who are willing to accept lower earnings in exchange for living in Colorado ("the sunshine tax"). Jonathan is extremely ambitious and frustrated that he's not earning what he would in other parts of the country. He's also envious of the opportunities for interesting IP work in places like Seattle, Austin, and the Silicon Valley. However, he doesn't like the idea of moving—he has a great condo and likes the 300 days of sunshine.

Starting Over

Ryan, who is in his early forties, has done extremely well as a tax partner in a major firm in Atlanta. In addition to earning good money, he has invested well and is quite comfortable financially. However, he is sick of his life. What he really wants to do is teach. He taught for two years between college and law school, and the experience was one of the highlights of his life. His ideal would be to teach in a private school. But he doesn't like the idea of starting a new career at age 46.

Each of these issues may reflect an important personal value—status, stability, recognition, etc. However, in each case the individual is in a quandary because he or she is unwilling to examine the value, or consider whether other values are more important. As a result, the person stays stuck.

Preconceptions about the Degree of Change We Need

Progress can also be blocked by preconceptions about how much change we actually need. This can take two forms: clinging to incremental steps when what we need is a bigger change, or insisting that only a major change can help us and therefore dismissing smaller yet potentially useful steps. Our insistence that change be of a certain magnitude is often rooted in unexamined assumptions about what we need or what is possible.

Choosing a Small Change When a Larger One Is Called For

Jack's passion has always been theater, television, and movies. He is a great writer and has a charismatic personality. His dream is to become a television writer. Jack found no satisfaction in corporate law and thought that he might be able to achieve his goals by working in entertainment law. So he moved to another firm that has some entertainment industry clients, for whom he occasionally drafts contracts, yet he is still doing legal work and is still unhappy.

Avoiding a Small Change When a Larger One Is Not Possible

Jacqueline, who graduated from an Ivy League law school, works for a small firm and has no prospects for upward mobility. Her days are long and stressful. Worse, her boss has a semityrannical, aggressive personality. Jacqueline rues the fact that she has not achieved the promise of her earlier years. Her friends suggest that she find another firm with a less toxic environment. However, Jacqueline doesn't want to just go to another firm, she wants to change her life entirely.

Exercise: Identify Your Taboos

Think of someone who knows you quite well and is familiar with the ways in which you feel stuck. (Consider one of the folks on your personal board of directors, discussed in chapter 6.) Ask this person the following questions:

1. What are some complaints that I make over and over?

2. What types of actions have I taken to deal with these problems?

3. What types of actions have I not taken?

4. What do I not want to hear?

5. How do I sell myself short?

Based on the responses you have gathered, what are some of your taboos?

Interrogating Your Taboos

Once you have identified your taboos, the task is to explore them—in other words, to reclassify an issue from a taboo to something that can be openly discussed and compared against other values. A good way to do this is to describe the action you might take, and then elaborate different scenarios—worst-case, likely, and best-case—of the potential outcome.

Janet, the unemployed consultant married to the unemployed banker above, considered the idea of her family downsizing its lifestyle. She explored that taboo by first describing the action she might take: "My husband and I take less-stressful, lower-paying jobs. We sell our home and buy a smaller one in our current town, or buy in another community entirely. Our children transfer to public school. We cut summer camp expenditures, stop taking elaborate vacations, and focus on paying off consumer debt and saving more money."

Based on that proposed action, she postulated three outcomes:

- *Worst-case scenario:* We hate the new house and town. Our relatives and former friends think we have really screwed up. Our kids hate their new school and develop behavioral problems. It takes a really long time for my husband and me to find jobs different from the ones we've left. I find my new career unstimulating and regret leaving the fast track. My husband and I fight a lot and ultimately divorce, causing long-term trauma to our children.

- *Most likely scenario:* It takes time and effort to sell our house, but it gets done. With a cheaper mortgage, our expenses drop dramatically. Our children are not happy about changing schools, but it's not the end of the world. Some of our friends drop us, but only the ones we didn't really like that much anyway. My husband and I learn to be conscious about money and not use it as a way to act out. Our health improves from working fewer hours. We spend more time with our kids, which is great but also a different kind of work. We feel good about living within our means and not always having the nagging idea that we need to earn more. Life is maybe more boring, but a lot more peaceful. We have some breathing room to figure things out.

- *Best-case scenario:* By leaving our current careers, we jump-start the process of finding work we actually like. We realize that work can be fun and fulfilling, not just a stressful thing you do to make money. By going to public schools, our children start becoming more grounded in the real world. They become less materialistic and narcissistic. Since my husband and I actually have more time to spend with them, we take a greater role in their educational and moral development and don't have to create perfect external opportunities (like private schools, trips to Europe, and expensive summer camps) as substitutes for parental involvement. We feel we have control in our lives, rather than just reacting to everything. We feel optimistic and young again.

What will be the actual outcome in Janet's life if she and her husband take the taboo action? It's impossible to predict. It could be that the outcome would include elements from all three scenarios. What this exploration does is to provide Janet with information she can use to figure out what kinds of actions make sense for her and her family.

You can never ensure good results, but you can strive to make good decisions. And the more open you are about exploring your own taboos, the better will be the decisions you make.

Exercise: Scenario Building

Consider one of your taboos—an option that you avoid putting on the table. Describe what this change would be. Then sketch out the worst-case, likely, and best-case scenarios for the outcome.

You might notice a tendency in the worst-case scenario to catastrophize, and in the best-case scenario to idealize. That's okay. It's the mix of the three scenarios that brings up greater truths.

Taboo Action: _____

_____

Worst-Case Scenario

_____

_____

_____

_____

_____

_____

Likely Scenario

_____

_____

_____

_____

_____

_____

Best-Case Scenario

_____

_____

_____

_____

_____

_____

Now, based on your three scenarios above, answer the following questions:

1. What are your main fears about the taboo action?

2. What are the potential payoffs?

3. What assumptions are you making?

4. What are some of the unknowns?

5. What's something you could do to check on how real these scenarios are, without committing yourself to a course of action you are not ready to take?

READING LIST

Maria Nemeth, *The Energy of Money*

Nemeth is a psychologist turned coach. She became motivated to explore this subject after she lost $35,000 in a business scam and ended up wondering how it was that an intelligent person could end up in such a bizarre financial situation. Her book is more an exploration of the psychological and spiritual factors that affect how we deal with money than a primer on how to get it or use it. It contains a number of useful exercises to get clear on your attitudes about and behaviors around money.

Joe Dominguez and Vicki Robin, *Your Money or Your Life: Transforming Your Relationship with Money and Achieving Financial Independence*

Tough love about money. The authors confront the reader with hard questions, including, If you're not in control of your financial situation now, what makes you think you ever will be? One of their most interesting exercises requires you to calculate your actual hourly income after making adjustments for long hours and all the additional expenditures you end up incurring when you don't have time to do anything yourself.

CHAPTER 14

The Creative Lawyer Unbound

There are a lot of things I would like to do with my life. Some of them I *have* done. Many I have not yet gotten to. (*Done*: Write a book. *Not done*: Become cover model for *Men's Health*.)

One of the things I have wanted to do for many years is to make some sense out of my experience of being a lawyer.

Like a lot of people—perhaps hundreds of thousands—I grew up thinking I would become a lawyer. However, when I actually became a lawyer, the experience wasn't quite what I had expected. Not bad, exactly, but different. Perhaps I thought that being a lawyer would take care of the question of being me. It didn't. The questions of "Who am I?" and "What am I supposed to be doing with my life?" continued to hover over me—and still do.

As I have said before, the process of creating a life that works for you does not unfold logically. It proceeds in fits and starts, involves unlearning as much as learning, and requires you to push forward amidst ambiguity. You have to act before you're ready to act, consider that your true interests and preferences might surprise you, and defer evaluation until you have collected a lot of evidence. You have to get out into the world, seek out new experiences, and connect with new people. I try to stick to these principles, not because they're always easy but because I've learned they work.

I've gone through lots of transitions myself. Some of them were fun and pleasant, and others painful and confusing. As a coach, I've had a fifth-row center seat to watch a lot of other people go through transitions, as well.

161

Among other things, I've noticed that it is possible for people to improve their lives, in particular their work lives. I've seen my clients' careers change from awful to good, and from good to thrilling. Maybe not in the first five seconds of trying, but with sustained effort, they have made meaningful changes.

Coaching can be very moving because you see what happens when blocked people become unblocked. In the coaching I do, the problem is not that clients are without capabilities. On the contrary, they are *filled* with capabilities. However, for whatever reasons, they are not fully accessing them. It's a beautiful thing to see them develop clarity, energy, and renewed excitement. And it's interesting, because rarely can I predict the exact direction they will move next.

I also see the positive benefits these transformations have on the wider world. Usually, when my clients find ways to make themselves happier and more satisfied in their careers, they make those around them happier, whether they spend their days doing tax strategy or teaching Gyrotonics. They end up contributing more to the world.

I've sometimes wondered: What would happen if even 1 percent of lawyers found better ways to express themselves, take care of themselves, and move forward? How much positive influence would they have? How much would they contribute to the world? A lot, I think.

So my goal is to help lawyers move forward.

You can do anything you want. And it will be great.

APPENDIX

Master Plan Template and Examples

Master Plan

VALUES AND VISION

My Values

Vision

GROWTH AND EXPLORATION

Competency Gap Analysis

Current competencies	Desired competencies

Learning Plan (Including Experiments)

Parallel growth goals	Other experiments

TOOLS AND RESOURCES
Positioning Statements (Version 1)   (Version 2)
Network Assessment *Strengths:* *Things to improve:*
Personal Board of Directors

SELF-MANAGEMENT
To manage my energy, given my preference for extroversion/ introversion, I will: *I'm aware of, and can live with, the following tradeoffs:*   *Things that violate my bottom line and that I will not tolerate are:*

Jane's Master Plan

VALUES AND VISION

My Values

- Growth (personal and professional)
- Hard work
- Community (giving back)
- Money
- Family
- Creating opportunities for others
- Civic involvement
- Efficiency

Vision

I'm still the executive director of the nonprofit I started leading five years ago. I am known for being an effective and fair manager and also for being an insightful, visionary leader. My organization is considered an exemplar for other legal nonprofits in terms of efficient operations, robust fundraising, creative programs, and strong PR. I continue to expand my own learning on leadership and management. Separately, I have become involved as an advisor and occasional small investor in local business and real estate projects, especially those involving women and minority entrepreneurs. Though I have a lot of professional responsibilities, I also have freedom to determine my schedule, which means that I can spend time with my family. My grandson invited me to speak at his elementary school's Career Day and I was a huge hit!

GROWTH AND EXPLORATION

Competency Gap Analysis

Current competencies	Desired competencies
<ul><li>Legal analysis</li><li>Budgeting and financial management</li><li>Writing and editing</li><li>Organizational skills</li><li>Professional demeanor</li><li>Strong professional network</li><li>Credibility with nonprofit world (from board positions, etc.)</li></ul>	<ul><li>Fundraising skills (getting the sale)</li><li>Donor and board management</li><li>Managing larger teams (including how to deal with poorly performing team members)</li><li>Best practices in operations</li><li>Real estate and small business metrics</li></ul>

Learning plan (Including Experiments)

Parallel growth goals	Other experiments
Simultaneously: (1) develop managerial and leadership skills for job as executive director; (2) explore real estate and small business investments to figure out best role and path for me	• Attend training at Foundation Center in New York • Join a leadership organization • Hire a consultant to do an assessment of strengths/weaknesses • Start hanging out with real estate people

TOOLS AND RESOURCES

Positioning Statements
(executive director role)
I'm the executive director of a regional nonprofit legal organization. I previously practiced law for nearly 25 years in a major financial institution. I love applying my legal and relationship-building skills toward the mission of my organization. I'm pursuing a self-study program to identify best practices in nonprofit management and make sure that I'm following them! I'm interested in learning how other executive directors handle their challenges, and what resources they use to get their job done.

(small business or real estate investor role)
I've worked as a corporate counsel for nearly 25 years. In that capacity I've handled all types of transactions, and I would say I have a very well-developed business and legal mind. One area I'm very interested in now is small-business development. I'm especially interested in entrepreneurial ventures, including real estate development, by women and minorities. I'd like to learn more about ways that I might become involved, perhaps as an advisor, an investor, or both.

Network Assessment
Strengths:

• I have an excellent legal network. My friends are a diverse lot and are in good places. I keep up with people.
• I also know a fair number of people in business, although I tend not to tap into these folks as much.

Things to improve:

• I tend to avoid asking for things. Obviously, this is not helpful when I am trying to raise money for my organization.

- I am overinvested in the lawyer world and underinvested in the small-business world. I need to stretch myself to reach into my "weak ties."

Personal Board of Directors

- Mary Ng, a friend since law school who knows me through and through
- My brother, who has always encouraged me to be a leader
- John Wyatt, a person I met at a new executive directors meeting who is also a lawyer and also wildly ambitious about making it in the non-profit world. I need that energy!
- Sumita, my one friend who has a gift for organizational politics

SELF-MANAGEMENT

To manage my energy given preference for extroversion/introversion, I will:

- Come to work half an hour early, so that I can plan my day when no one is here
- Leave the office for lunch (so that I avoid shoptalk over sandwiches)
- Allow myself one hour each evening for reading
- When going to conferences, try to be a speaker or panelist rather than attendee, since the former is actually easier for me (I like clear roles) than the latter

I'm aware of, and can live with, the following tradeoffs:

- I love being around smart, professional people *and* for the time-being, I'm somewhat isolated in my job.
- I really enjoyed my previous job *and* I do not want to go back.
- I am accustomed to being extremely successful in my work *and* I am underdeveloped in certain skill areas.
- I can see specific development needs for me right now *and* I need to communicate compet ence to my Board.

Things that violate my bottom line and which I will not tolerate are:

- When I am cut off from things that make me happy, like reading, plays, and music. I will make time to do these things, even if I have to go back to the office later!
- If I conclude, based on good evidence, that my organization is not succeeding in its social mission, I will leave and find something else.

George's Master Plan

My values

- Financial success
- Entrepreneurship
- Being a good husband
- Being a good father
- Self-improvement

- Hard work
- Physical health
- Competitive sports
- Living in New York City and being real

Vision

I'm the owner of a business that imports interesting products from overseas to the U.S. I work very hard but have a lot of variety in my professional life—I come up with new ideas, manage a team of good people, travel from time to time, and am out of the office doing marketing and sales. My marriage is good, and my child is healthy. My salary is lower than at the law firm, but there is a large potential upside in the event things really take off. In exchange for this financial risk, I have more freedom. My several years of working for a law firm helped create the foundation for this work by teaching me about business, improving my judgment, and establishing financial security. My former colleagues at the firm still like me, and some of them are minority investors in my company.

Competency Gap Analysis

Current competencies	Desired competencies
• Writing and editing	• Strong legal analysis skills
• Research	• Negotiation experience
• Hard work, professional standards	• Experience managing teams
• Sense of reality	• Financial analysis
• Good networking attitude	• Broader set of data about entrepreneurial opportunities
• Entrepreneurial spirit	• Knowledge of venture capital/ private equity world
• I know what I don't know	

Learning plan (Including Experiments)

Parallel growth goals	Other experiments
Simultaneously develop: (1) legal skills and credibility; (2) managerial and leadership skills; (3) connections to entrepreneurs and businesspeople	• Seek out assignments working with start-up clients • Take training as offered by the firm • Go to a work/life balance seminar with my wife • Be a sounding board for friends who are engaged in entrepreneurial ventures

TOOLS AND RESOURCES

Positioning Statements

(internal professional development version)

I'm an associate in the structured finance group at the firm. Right now I'm focusing on improving my legal skills, as well as my knowledge of the business principles that underlie the work we do. I am also interested in how people manage work/life balance along the way to becoming partners at the firm. I would like to learn more about how your own career has developed here.

(improve business network version)

I'm a corporate associate at a major firm in midtown Manhattan. I'm interested in the business terms behind deals, and I like working with teams of people. I've always had strong business interests, and in high school I ran a very profitable Pokemon card trading business. [For clients:] I'd love to learn more about what you do, as it would help me be more effective when I am working on projects for you. [For general contacts:] I'm interested in meeting people who are developing ideas for entrepreneurial ventures. I have a good legal and business mind and might be a good resource for them.

Network Assessment

Strengths:

- It's easy for me to speak to people I don't know very well.
- I know people from all walks of life—I grew up on the Lower East Side and attended public schools and people think I am real (not pretentious).

170

Things to improve:

- I don't know enough professional people—this part of my life is just beginning.
- I need to have more focused communications so that I don't sound like a high school student.
- I need to be strategic so I don't just end up meeting lawyers.
- That being said, I would like to establish more meaningful relationships with people at work so that they know who I am as a person, and vice-versa.

Personal Board of Directors

- My wife
- John Norton (supervisor from my summer working at the city prosecutor's office)
- Professor Park from law school (he thinks I have a good legal mind)
- Jennifer Skorzy (friend from college who has already been in three start-up companies)
- My mom (knows a lot about financial management)

SELF-MANAGEMENT

To manage my energy given preference for extroversion/introversion, I will:

- Take a 15-minute walk every day at lunch
- Try participating in the law firm's intramural program
- Call my wife or a friend twice a day for short conversations
- Participate in my daughter's kindergarten reading group

I'm aware of, and can live with, the following tradeoffs:

- I want to make fast progress *and* my firm is a hierarchical place where I have to pay my dues.
- I am making good money *and* my wife and I have to watch our spending to make sure we save it.
- I ultimately want to go into business *and* for the next several years I will be focusing on being a good lawyer.
- I need a lot of stimulation *and* my job requires that I spend large amounts of time by myself perusing somewhat boring documents.

Things that violate my bottom line and which I will not tolerate are:

- If I am not able to balance doing well at work with having a decent family life, I will get another job, even if it is lower paying and less prestigious.
- If I start to lose my personality and forget why I am here, I will leave.
- If I go through a long period of time without learning, I will make a change.

Nicole's Master Plan

My Values

Being my authentic self category!	Making it category!
• Writing and self-expression • Dance and physical health • Being a free spirit • Travel • Creative contribution • Getting ahead	• Professionalism • Personal power • Working with smart people • Recognition for my talents and work ethic

Vision

I run a talent agency with offices in Los Angeles and New York, like a small, elite version of Endeavor. I have a group of interesting, thoughtful, and *fun* people working with me, and our clients include a lot of celebrities who are materially successful but also spiritually advanced. This business is the perfect combination of my own background in dance and the arts along with my legal and business training. My clients like me because I can support their artistic development *and* run no-nonsense meetings with tough studio executives where I know all the power lingo. My years spent working in marketing for the law firm helped to make this happen because it offered a solid platform for me to develop my skills and enough freedom to create my own network. I have an exciting husband, and two trilingual children. Because I dance regularly, I look great. Once a year, our whole family goes on a detoxifying yoga retreat to Costa Rica.

Competency Gap Analysis

Current competencies	Desired competencies
• Writing and editing • Organizational skills • Emotional intelligence • Smart • Strange ability to meet and chat up celebrities • Beginnings of specialized marketing knowledge • Positive energy!	• Strong marketing skills • People management (being more of a manager than a friend) • Experience contracting and deal-making in the arts world • Personal financial management • Thicker skin

Learning plan (Including Experiments)

Parallel growth goals	Other experiments
Simultaneously develop: (1) legal marketing skills; (2) upward management; (3) connections to the entertainment world and relevant legal/business	• Start representing undiscovered actors, dancers, and artists in New York • Attend the Sundance Film Festival • Join a board to develop management skills and connections • Take performance classes

TOOLS AND RESOURCES

Positioning Statements
(professional development version)
I'm a marketing manager for a major law firm based in Los Angeles. What I love about my job is that I'm able to use my knowledge of how law firms work—based on my previous experience practicing law—while adding my own abilities in creative marketing and client management. This is a great niche for me, and I want to learn everything there is to know about marketing professional services!

(talent agent version)
I've had two different careers: as a professional dancer and as a lawyer. Unlikely as it sounds, there is one factor that both careers have in common: they both involve marketing the services of highly capable people. My goal is to launch my own representation agency. Right now, I'm working pro bono with a couple of fledgling actors in Los Angeles to help get their careers launched. I'm thrilled at how much they are progressing. I'm going to New York next month and would love to meet either aspiring actors or working agents to talk shop. Let's take a meeting!

Network Assessment
Strengths:

• I know a lot of people (I'm a connector in the Malcolm Gladwell sense).
• I'm able to chat up senior and even famous people very easily.
• I'm a good addition to groups—for professionals, I'm "interesting"; for artists, I'm "professional."

Things to improve:

- My network of people who are actually talent agents or studio people is very limited.
- While I meet many people, I'm not sure how effective my conversations are. I need to work on follow-through.

Personal Board of Directors

- Tim K (Calvin Klein model I met at a party who graduated Phi Beta Kappa from UT Austin)
- Flora Costantini (mentor who hired me who left to take bigger job at another firm)
- Jerry Clark (my accountant, who sounds like a character on *The Sopranos* but is smart and keeps me grounded)
- Elizabeth King (gives the best advice about relationships)

SELF-MANAGEMENT

To manage my energy given preference for <u>extroversion</u>/*introversion, I will:*

- Pay for a one-year membership to the Caporeira dance studio
- Put myself in structured environments (like classes) where I meet people
- Enjoy chatting with support staff every morning, without feeling guilty about it being nonbillable
- Get a massage once a month

I'm aware of, and can live with, the following tradeoffs:

- I am trying to break into a tough industry in an unconventional way *and* I have always done things my way!
- I want each one of my days to be filled with excitement *and* I have many days when I need to just clock in and do the job.

Things that violate my bottom line and which I will not tolerate are:

- If I find myself falling into a negativity spiral at work (the way I did in law school), I will find another job.
- If I am hanging out with people who disparage my ambitions or who don't get who I am at this stage in my life, I will find new friends.

INDEX

ABOUT THE AUTHOR

MICHAEL MELCHER is an attorney who is one of the country's leading career coaches. With a blend of humor, sensitivity and professional acumen, he has helped hundreds of individuals transform their careers into personal platforms that are professionally fulfilling and personally meaningful. A gifted speaker and workshop leader, he has addressed audiences on career development themes across the United States as well as in Europe and Asia.

MICHAEL is a graduate of Harvard College, Stanford Law School, and the Stanford Graduate School of Business. He worked for several years as an associate at Davis Polk & Wardwell in New York, was previously a Foreign Service Officer in Calcutta and Taipei, ran an internet start-up in Silicon Valley, and is currently a partner at Next Step Partners, the leadership development and executive coaching firm. He has lived and worked in five countries and speaks Spanish and Mandarin Chinese. *The Creative Lawyer* is his second book.

http://www.michaelmelcher.com
http://www.thecreativelawyer.com